OUT IN ★ ★ ★ ★
CHICAGO

LGBT HISTORY AT THE CROSSROADS

Jill Austin and Jennifer Brier, editors

Chicago **History** Museum

CHICAGO

Chicago History Museum
1601 North Clark Street
Chicago, Illinois 60614-6038
www.chicagohistory.org

ISBN: 978-0-913820-35-3

Director of Print and Multimedia Publications: Rosemary K. Adams
Designed by Eileen Wagner Design

The exhibition *Out in Chicago* was on display in the
Bessie Green-Field Warshawsky Gallery, The Mazza Foundation Gallery,
and The Benjamin Benedict Green-Field Gallery of The Pritzker
Foundation Special Exhibition Wing at the Chicago History Museum
from May 21, 2011 through March 26, 2012.

The Elizabeth Morse and Elizabeth Morse Genius Charitable Trusts
were the presenting sponsors of *Out in Chicago*.

Out in Chicago Lead Corporate Sponsor: Northern Trust

Additional support provided by The Chicago Community Trust;
The Pauls Foundation; Sara Lee Foundation; Polk Bros. Foundation;
The Richard H. Driehaus Foundation; Goodworks Fund; UBS;
NIB Foundation; Northwestern University; and the Ellen Stone Belic
Institute for the Study of Women and Gender in the Arts and Media,
Columbia College Chicago.

Individual support provided by Robert Kohl and Clark Pellett,
Art Johnston and Jose Peña, Charles R. Middleton and John S. Geary,
Greg Cameron and Greg Thompson, Shawn Donnelley, Robbin Burr,
Patrick M. Sheahan, and Esther Saks.

Exhibition created in partnership with UIC College of Liberal Arts &
Sciences, and Center on Halsted. Additional assistance from Community
Marketing Inc, WFMT and WTTW Chicago Public Television,
WBEZ Chicago Public Radio, The Fairmont Hotel, and River North
Sales & Service.

CONTENTS

PREFACE

While the media has focused public attention on the debate about gays in the military and its "don't ask, don't tell" policy, another parallel practice has gone virtually unnoticed: mainstream history museums have, with almost no exceptions, excluded lesbian, gay, bisexual, and transgender (LGBT) communities from the local, state, regional, and national narratives they present to the public in their exhibitions.[1] Indeed, history museums have tacitly practiced their own version of "don't ask, don't tell."[2]

In 1999, I attended a session at the American Association of Museums annual meeting in Seattle that focused on the question: Why are libraries willing to present public exhibitions on LGBT people and their history, but museums are not?[3] One member of the audience offered the insightful observation that the public views libraries as sources of information, but looks to museums for truth. It seems that we can accept, even celebrate, library exhibitions on LGBT history because they are no less or no more important than any other form of information; but without the imprimatur of veracity, authority, and finality that museums bestow they fall short of the gravitas LGBT communities desire.

Museums, which have grown ever more sensitive to the desires and needs of the public, as well as to ticket sales, might argue that LGBT history exhibitions are simply not compelling to mainstream museum audiences. But another way to put it is that museums are unwilling to risk presenting the fundamental truth that despite a long history of discrimination, prejudice, and repression in America, LGBT people have nevertheless made fulfilling and loving lives in same-sex relationships. More than simply bucking popular trends, accepting this basic tenet defies prevailing social myths and negative stereotypes that LGBT people are abnormal, perverse, and threaten the American way of life. And while gay and lesbian characters have become commonplace, even popular, in films and television, changes we tout as evidence of how tolerant Americans have become, they still remain absent from almost every history museum.

Museum exhibitions are thus a critical litmus test of our willingness as a society to accept LGBT people as full partners in determining not only their own lives but also in shaping the future of America. History museums have a unique opportunity to play a pivotal role in presenting the history of LGBT people to the public to help them overcome the prevailing myths, negative stereotypes, and fear that dominate our interaction with LGBT communities. *Out in Chicago* seeks to help move us in that direction.

The path that led the Chicago History Museum (CHM) to organizing *Out in Chicago* is not linear; instead, it is long, meandering, and sometimes obscure. Archie Motley, who served as archivist at CHM from 1960 until his retirement in 1998 and built the Museum's impressive urban history archive of Chicago, was a pioneer in establishing this direction. A champion of diversity in all of his activities at CHM, Motley's values are most clearly seen in his acquisition work and the legacy of inclusiveness that defines this extraordinary archival collection. He collected papers that crossed class, race, and gender boundaries and represented individuals and organizations engaged in community advocacy, neighborhood work, labor relations, and faith-based initiatives.

As part of this effort, he acquired the Pearl Hart papers (1942–72) in 1976. Hart, an attorney and a lesbian, was a passionate defender of civil rights cases and a leader in leftist political organizations. She was revered for her efforts to stop discrimination against gays and lesbians; the Gerber/Hart Library and Archives is named in her honor. In 1987, Motley acquired two additional collections that anchored CHM as an important resource for Chicago LGBT history. The Gregory Sprague papers (1972–87) are a treasure trove of material collected and created by one of the city's earliest historians of gay life in Chicago, including items related to his classes for the Lavender University, later called the Chicago Gay and Lesbian History Project. Also in 1987, U.S. District Court Judge Susan Getzendanner placed the Chicago Police Department Red Squad and related records at CHM to ensure they would not be destroyed and to preserve them as historical documents. These records, which offer detailed reports on the activities of Chicagoans identified as potential political subversives, include materials related to gay and lesbian activists in the city. The gay and lesbian archival material Motley collected for CHM complemented the more extensive and broader collection of the Gerber/Hart Library and Archives founded in 1981 as the Midwest Gay and Lesbian Archives and Library. Gerber/Hart and CHM have been important stops for scholars researching Chicago's LGBT history.

CHM and the Gerber/Hart Library and Archives were more than complimentary organizations. Beginning in 1992, they partnered to present the city's LGBT history by collaborating on the exhibition *Day Without History*, organized in recognition of World's AIDS Day, which was on view at CHM from November 27 to December 5. In January 1993, Gerber/Hart Library and Archives and CHM cosponsored a lecture by Alan Berube on "Gay and Lesbian Life in World War II," in conjunction with the CHM exhibition *Chicago Goes to War*. And CHM and Gerber/Hart collaborated to bring *The Advocate*–sponsored exhibition *Long Road to Freedom: A History of the Gay and Lesbian Movement in America*, which was on view at CHM from October 7 to November 12, 1995. A small group of Gerber/Hart Library and Archives materials was also exhibited to complement *Long Road,* which was CHM's first exhibition on Chicago's LGBT communities.

Out at CHM (originally called *Out at CHS*) came to fruition in 2003, when members of the LGBT communities approached the Museum about having an ongoing program about their history in a mainstream institution. The goal was to build a new diverse audience for CHM, to foster a new body of historical scholarship on Chicago's LGBT communities, and to address the communities' members' lack of historical knowledge about the evolution of the city's queer residents. George Chauncey, professor of history and director of the Lesbian and Gay Studies Project at the University of Chicago, played a key role in defining the intellectual agenda of the program and in bringing the support of the Project and the University of Chicago. Board members and supporters of the Center on Halsted, including James Alexander, Greg Cameron, Evette Cardona, Robert Kohl, Vicki Raymont, and Patrick Sheahan gave enthusiastic support to this initiative and brought the critical endorsement of the Center.

Over the next eight years, the scope of the program broadened as did support. Jennifer Brier and Jay Grossman followed George Chauncey in providing intellectual leadership for the program, and their respective universities, the University of Illinois at Chicago, College of Liberal Arts & Sciences, and Northwestern University's Weinberg College of Arts and Sciences, along with the Ellen Stone Belic Institute for the Study of Women and Gender in the Arts and Media, Columbia College Chicago, brought critical support to ensure the longevity of the program. Joshua Eisenberg and Elizabeth Garibay managed the program for CHM. The idea of doing an exhibition at CHM on the history of Chicago's LGBT people was a goal from the very beginning of discussions, but scholarship had not progressed far enough along to support this effort. Now, eight years later, this publication and exhibition are a testament to the original vision of documenting and making the most current scholarship on the history of Chicago's LGBT communities accessible to a broader public.

Out in Chicago, the exhibition and this book, would not have been possible without the critical support from Chicago foundations, corporations, and individuals. The Elizabeth Morse and Elizabeth Morse Genius Charitable Trusts are the presenting sponsors of *Out in Chicago*. Lead corporate sponsor for the exhibition is Northern Trust. Additional support is provided by The Chicago Community Trust, The Pauls Foundation, Polk Bros. Foundation, Sara Lee Foundation, The Richard H. Driehaus Foundation, Goodworks Fund, UBS, NIB Foundation, Northwestern University, and the Ellen Stone Belic Institute for the Study of Women and Gender in the Arts and Media, Columbia College Chicago. Individual support is provided by Robert Kohl and Clark Pellett, Art Johnston and Jose Peña, Charles R. Middleton and John S. Geary, Greg Cameron and Greg Thompson, Shawn Donnelley, Robbin Burr, Patrick M. Sheahan, and Esther Saks. The exhibition was created in partnership with the University of Illinois at Chicago College of Liberal Arts & Sciences and the Center on Halsted.

Special thanks to the Gerber/Hart Library and Archives (celebrating its thirtieth anniversary) and Karen Sendziak for their pioneering work in documenting the lives and struggles of Chicago LGBT communities, for an ongoing partnership with the Chicago History Museum, for opening the Library's wonderful holdings to the exhibition co-curators, and for generously loaning so many of the Library's documents and artifacts for the *Out in Chicago* exhibition.

Every exhibition and publication project of this scale requires years of planning and dedicated staff to develop and review the major components to ensure that every small detail is addressed, and this effort is no different. Three individuals deserve special recognition. Jill Austin and Jennifer Brier, co-curators of the *Out in Chicago* exhibition and co-editors of this publication, formed into a remarkable team that created a provocative and compelling interpretation of Chicago's LGBT history based on new scholarship anchored in the intersection of urban history with the evolution of sexual and gender identity. Their sustained and personal engagement with LGBT communities, their insistence on achieving the highest scholarly standards, their efforts to address diversity honestly and clearly, their respect for their colleagues, and their unbridled enthusiasm for history are the hallmarks of an incredible commitment to the power of history to change people's lives, and this book and exhibition reflect their brilliant, path-breaking scholarship and their dedication to compelling public history. I also want to give special thanks and recognition to Gary T. Johnson, president of the Chicago History Museum, who championed this project throughout the city from the beginning. His unflinching support for this book and exhibition has been inspiring, and without his personal commitment to preserving and presenting the diverse stories of Chicago as central aspects of CHM's educational mission, neither this publication or the exhibition would have been possible.

The co-curators had the good fortune to work with an awesome core team, as well as the extraordinary efforts of a talented and dedicated staff. They were assisted by Anne Parsons and Jessica Herczeg-Konecny during the research and implementation phases of this project; their commitment to the project and the work ethic they embodied far exceeded all expectations. The staff exhibition team developed creative solutions to all aspects of the exhibition and ensured that the team met its goals. Daniel Oliver worked closely with co-curators Austin and Brier on the exhibition design to ensure the narrative threads had visual impact, and the exhibition themes were choreographed to create a powerful learning experience. Emily Nordstrom brought her uncommon understanding of the power of language and advocacy for the visitor to the editing of the exhibition labels; Mark Ramirez designed striking graphics to guide the visitor thorough the galleries. Liz Garibay developed a compelling array of public programs that focus on key aspects of the history of Chicago's LGBT communities. Rosemary Adams served dual roles as project manager, overseeing the budget, schedule, and the progress of the exhibition team, and as editor of this publication. Her experience managing many CHM exhibitions over the past five years ensured that the planning and implementation phases unfolded smoothly, and her extensive experience in editing and book production were key to achieving this important book. Phyllis Rabineau oversaw all aspects of the exhibition, offering sound guidance at critical points in its development, encouraging the staff to be innovative, and helping to solve problems large and small. Tamara Biggs oversaw production of the video greeters and the video interviews of members of the LGBT communities.

I offer my sincere gratitude to all CHM staff, volunteers, and Trustees, whose ongoing efforts provide a foundation that enables the Museum to support the kind of original research that has made *Out in Chicago* possible.

Russell Lewis
Executive Vice President
and Chief Historian

ENDNOTES

1. The 2005 exhibition, *The Unspoken Past: Atlanta Lesbian and Gay History, 1940-1970*, at the Atlanta History Center is one of the very few exceptions.

2. This does not include a range of museums devoted to LGBT history. The National Holocaust Museum in Washington, D.C. focuses on homosexuals as one of the groups the Nazis targeted for extermination in World War II.

3. *Becoming Visible: The Legacy of Stonewall* opened in June 1994 at the New York Public Library and broke attendance records. Two years later, *Public Faces/Private Lives* opened in May at the Boston Public Library and broke attendance records. In 1998, the James C. Hormel Gay and Lesbian Center at the San Francisco Public Library opened the exhibition *Harvey Milk, Second Sight*. In June 2009, the New York Public Library opened the exhibition *1969: The Year of Gay Liberation*.

OUT IN ✶ ✶ ✶ ✶
CHICAGO

OUT IN CHICAGO
Exhibiting LGBT History
at the Crossroads

Jill Austin and Jennifer Brier

Out in Chicago chronicles how urban dwellers, since the formation of the city of Chicago, have organized their lives around their sexual desires and senses of self. The exhibition covers a wide span of time, from the period before the terms lesbian, gay, bisexual, and transgender (LGBT) existed, to today's conversations about queer identity and gender ambiguity. *Out in Chicago* explores sexual and gender history as urban history. Cities have long been spaces both of nonconformity and conformity, anonymity and identification. They are places where people who may be travelers, migrants, immigrants, wanderers can get lost in the crowd or escape rejection by a spouse or family, or find acceptance with others more like themselves. The crowds, the jobs, the meeting places in the city allow for different sexual expressions and gender identities, each of which fosters communities that might not exist in smaller towns and rural areas.[1] Chicago, as the quintessential city of industry and ambition, city at the crossroads of America, haven for migrants, matters to this sexual history as much as the coastal, and more studied, cities of San Francisco and New York. Newcomers arrived in Chicago looking to create a place for themselves, where they could make new friends who shared their sexuality and interests informed by it.

Since its incorporation as a city in 1837, Chicago has been a queer space. For example, the city's location as an endpoint for immigration in the nineteenth century and for the black migration from the South in the first half of the twentieth century made certain kinds of sexual and gender expression possible. With the arrival of hundreds of thousands of African Americans over the course of the first decades of the twentieth century alongside immigrants from all over the globe, a racially integrated club scene emerged in the city's Levee district, one that seemed welcoming to those who acted on same-sex desire. Throughout the exhibition, we place the history of sexuality into a larger discussion with other critical aspects of Chicago's past, most particularly the history of class and race relations, to try to tell stories that have not been heard as well as retell those that have become trite.[2]

Out in Chicago is, in essence, a *queer* history of Chicago as an urban center. We use the term *queer* to signify a rejection of the normal or normative in relation to sexuality and gender. On the one hand queer serves as a shorthand for LGBT, allowing us to talk about lesbians, gay men, bisexuals, and transgender people in one word. On the other hand, queer is distinct from LGBT, an acronym signifying a group of historically specific identities. Queer allows us to talk about people who did not identify as lesbian, gay, bisexual, or transgender, but nonetheless had same-sex desire or expressed their gender in defiant ways.

We were surely not the first to think of this model of historical analysis. Our ability to present a museum-based queer narrative of Chicago's LGBT past was made possible by major developments taking place in historical institutions across the country. Historically, the few large-scale LGBT exhibitions that have been displayed have appeared in public libraries, such as the New York Public Library's 1994 *Becoming Visible: The Legacy of Stonewall* and more recently *Out at the Library* at the Hormel Center in the San Francisco Public Library mounted in 2005. More modest—but no less significant—work in local history appeared at the Hennepin Historical Society in Minneapolis, the Atlanta History Center, and as this essay was going to press, the first GLBT history museum was opening in San Francisco, under the auspices of the GLBT Historical Society. Some non-museum organizations, most notably OutHistory.org, have initiated online exhibits, bringing LGBT history to online publics.[3]

Beyond these national efforts, Chicago has long been home to a budding LGBT history scene. Several community-based historical institutions, including the Gerber/Hart Library and Archives, the Leather Archives and Museum, and the Hull-House Museum, keep queer history on display year round, and a few "mainstream" institutions have run LGBT history exhibitions: in 1995, the Chicago History Museum (CHM) partnered with Gerber/Hart to display *The Long Road to Freedom*, a traveling show that documented the *Advocate*'s first twenty-five years; the two institutions would collaborate on programming for a Day Without History, a project to acknowledge how the

HIV/AIDS epidemic has mattered to public history. In 2000, the University of Chicago ran *Homosexuality in the City: A Century of Research at the University of Chicago*, in its Regenstein Library. Chicago has also enjoyed its fair share of documentaries and publications centered on LGBT history over the past few years, including *Out and Proud in Chicago*, a book edited and published by journalist Tracy Baim and a film produced by WTTW Channel 11. Filmmaker Ron Pajak's documentary, *Quearborn & Perversion*, also explores LGBT bar culture in the city.

Despite our embarrassment of riches in terms of LGBT public history, some of our most powerful insights for how to bring LGBT history into dialogue with the Chicago History Museum and its permanent collections and exhibitions came from within the walls of the museum itself. We found inspiration in Fred Wilson's *Mining the Museum* installations, a project that ran at the Maryland Historical Society in Baltimore from 1992 to 1993. *Mining the Museum* questioned how the institution had represented race through its collection and exhibition processes. Wilson juxtaposed the museum's collection of family heirlooms with objects used to proffer hate. For instance, Wilson interrogated portraits of white, affluent families that the historical society had displayed for years. In the past, the curators had asked visitors to focus their attention on the white figures in the painting, ignoring the African Americans who stood in the background. Wilson called the visitors' attention to the African Americans in the painting by using spotlights and audio effects to urge people to think about the presence and identities of the black figures.

3

In our case, mining the museum meant looking at objects that had previously been on display at CHM through the lens of race, gender, and sexuality. Just as Wilson found powerful examples in portraiture, we too found curatorial opportunities in a trove of oil paintings from CHM's collection that had hung in Chapin and Gore, a men's bar with several locations, popular in the early twentieth century. Most striking was the portrait of George Ade and Orson Wells that had served as the cover art for the catalogue of CHM's exhibition, *Big Picture* (fig. 1). Initially used as a representative example of Chicago art in the museum's collection—Ade was a major literary figure in turn-of-the-century Chicago, and Wells was his companion—we viewed the painting as displaying cross-dressing and hints at same sex desire. The "C" in a circle on the fan in Wells's hand refers not just to the Chicago Cubs, but to the Chicago Athletic Association, a male-only club and residence that was infamous for being a place where men could find and have sex with other men.[4] Our reinterpretation of the painting's details, shown here as it appeared in the gallery, is central to our story of how Chicago became queer and how Chicago, as a city, affected the shape of queer life (fig. 2).

Our approach to mining the collection to detail the connection between LGBT/queer history and Chicago history found its ultimate confirmation in our conversations with members of the LGBT community during a series of in-depth discussion with visitors. These "visitor panels" became the driving force behind the organization of the exhibition around themes rather than strict chronology.[5] At the same time, the visitor panels reminded us that to effectively tell the history of people with same-sex desire and gender nonconformity in Chicago we had to resist the temptation to look only for contemporary representations of LGBT in the past and instead work on exhibiting a range of sexual identities and gender expressions in their larger urban context.

In the essay that follows, we detail the four sections that form *Out in Chicago*. We begin with a discussion of why and how the physical body matters to LGBT urban history and urban identity; move to a section that details the evolution of the queer family and kinship circles, and the importance and problem of home for LGBT people in the past and present; turn to an extended display of how LGBT people have built community spaces throughout the city of Chicago; and end with a series of vignettes on the queer body politic. Using a model that takes us from the smallest social unit to the largest, we hope that the sections speak to each other and relate to the whole of Chicago history (fig. 3).

4

Section One: LGBT at the Crossroads

The opening section of *Out in Chicago* explores the relationship between gender—being male, female, or gender ambiguous—sexuality and the city. It explores how LGBT people, communities, and history came to be here, by introducing a range of individual urban residents, past and present, to detail the evolution of gender crossing. We begin in 1851, when the budding frontier city passed legislation prohibiting the public appearance of someone dressed in clothing "not of his or her sex" and fining violators a huge sum. We then explore what it meant, personally and publicly, to experiment with one's gender and how some people blurred the lines of living as an obvious, physically identifiable female or male. In many cases, we found people who inhabited a unique gender category that reflected male and female sensibilities.[6] We consider the range of ways people have comported themselves, whether

Figure 1. Caricature of George Ade and Orson Collins Wells, by William Herman Schmedtgen, 1912. CHM, gift of Charles H. Hermann.

Figure 2. Ade and Wells tabletop.

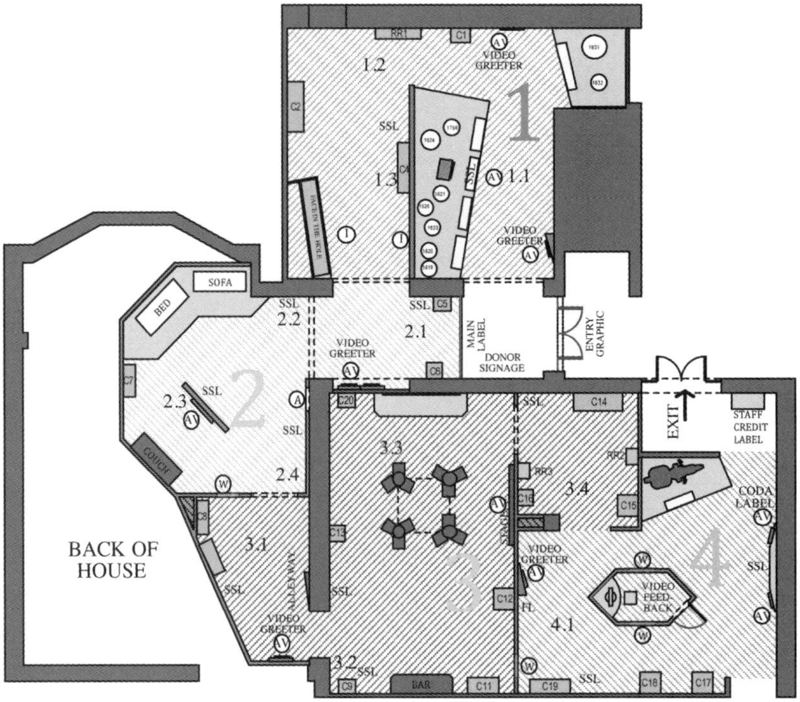

Figure 3. *Out in Chicago* floorplan, 2011.

in terms of how they dress, how they verbally identify themselves, or who they socialize with. Sexuality, gender expression, and gender identity are all part of the broader history of Chicago. These tales from across the city range from accounts of flamboyant escapades of performance artists to the everyday experience of life as an anonymous person on the streets looking for someone who shared same-sex desire.

We turned to the archives to see what the collection of digitized Chicago newspapers would tell us about the depth of LGBT and queer practices in this city. Imagine our surprise when we found hundreds of examples in the past of gender crossing even though (or perhaps because) Chicago was one of the first cities in the nation to institute a ban on cross dressing in 1851. The material we found in the Chicago press became the basis for the article in this collection by Jennifer Brier and Anne Parsons, and then became just one subsection in the exhibition's introductory section. The change in the material's status from the central story to one of many grew out of our conversations with the LGBT visitor panel. LGBT visitors wanted us to concentrate on the contemporary gender queer movement so that we could explore the development of identities based on sexual and gender ambiguity rather than rigid notion of male or female or heterosexual and homosexual. They also asked us to address how people with a range of sexual identities expressed, and continue to express, their gender. What we came to, in response to their interests and our sense of what we needed to detail for the exhibition to remain historical, was to explore why gender matters to LGBT history, and what that looked like in the urban dynamic of Chicago.

These individual efforts never occurred in a vacuum, so we also explore how various kinds of societal forces have made life for nonconformers difficult. These forces took many different forms such as turn-of-the-twentieth-century scientists, based in Chicago, who forcibly tried to define the actions of gender crossers by naming them "sexual inverts," people who took on the opposite gender so that they could realize same-sex attraction as a kind of heterosexuality. The legal system, too, has continuously invented prohibitions on cross dressing. In this section, we want *Out in Chicago* visitors to see the push/pull of what it means to express your gender or sexuality in ways not supported or envisioned by dominant society. By showing how people have consciously shaped their gender identity and appearance, often in contradiction to the law, this section speaks to how Chicago became a city where people who resisted gender conventions found a place to live their lives in and out of the shadows.

Even within (and beyond) the spectrum of identities ranging from L to G to B to T, for example, there are many ways to be and see others, and those distinctions are only made more complicated when thinking about the past as well. Language and lexicon—what words you use or claim to describe yourself and create an identity or perhaps challenge societal norms—play an important role in Chicago's history and therefore became a theme threaded through the entire gallery. In each section of the exhibition, we provide historical definitions of key terms related to the history of gender and sexuality, including queer, homosexual, and transgender, to name only a few.

Section Two: Are You Family?
The second section of the exhibition benefited from a summer afternoon's discussion with John D'Emilio, Adam Green, Ann Durkin Keating, and Amy Tyson, all leading Chicago scholars on issues and events that ground the current historical interpretation of the city in the post–World War II era. At the session, we asked the group what we needed to cover to shed the clearest (and queerest)

light on Chicago's LGBT history in the second half of the twentieth century. We owe a tremendous debt to this conversation for grounding the themes and experiences of the section in ways we had not expected, particularly in terms of public housing, urban housing developments, and migrations often based on race, class, and the myth of the nuclear family.

"Are You Family?" begins with the question of how Chicago's LGBT people have crafted families based on affectionate, romantic, and erotic love, and how they have built homes in the past. We were increasingly drawn to the idea of home—what it means to make a home and form different kinds of families and bonding relationships. Who makes a family? What makes a home? By examining the challenges of creating a home, sometimes in a hostile environment, this section considers the strategies that members of the LGBT community have deployed to build spaces of refuge and kinship in this city. After consulting with our scholars' group and receiving positive feedback from our visitor panel, we delved further into the idea of homes, housing, and companionship, rooted in specific architecture and place in the city as well as in experiences of immigration, migration and industry in nineteenth- and early twentieth-century Chicago.

This section explores questions of making family by suggesting the importance of both same-sex relationships and class position. We explore how settlements like Hull-House offered comforts of home to residents that went beyond the thin metal cots often found in boarding and rooming houses of the day. Despite the Spartan accommodations, we also consider how these all-male or all-female spaces made it possible for men and men or women and women to become fast friends. The two male railroad workers shown here in a friendly embrace suggest that working class men, regardless of their sexuality, found a kind of freedom in turn-of-the-century Chicago. Men of means, as was likely the case in the ink drawing by *Chicago Tribune* editorial cartoonist John T. McCutcheon, had a different kind of freedom than the Pullman strikers, one that allowed them to share an affectionate connection in public spaces such as the trolley car. We contrast the experience of working-class queer people with middle- and upper-class queer people to ask that visitors consider how gender, sexuality, and class affected one another throughout Chicago's history (fig. 4 and fig. 5).

Two essays included in this book, both print versions of popular *Out at CHM* presentations from the same evening, relate to the discussion of the early history of companionship and the making of non-normative families. Jay Grossman revisits the romantic and explicitly sexual, friendships of Walt

Figure 4. Two men during the Pullman Railroad strike,1894. CHM, ICHi-04917.

Whitman and argues that there was an American political dimension to Whitman's sexuality. Victoria Bissell Brown recalls an imaginary conversation she had with Jane Addams that inspired her original talk at the museum, and expands her thoughts on queerness (or lack thereof) and sexual ambiguity in turn-of-the-twentieth-century Chicago.

As the city evolved over the course of the twentieth century, housing, city planning, and racially segregated neighborhoods, all familiar topics of Chicago history, came to matter in terms of where LGBT people could settle, what kinds of home they could create, and with whom they could or could not live. Public policy and lucrative real estate developments, which, incidentally, helped give birth to Boystown as the city's "gay" neighborhood, targeted specific demographics that excluded LGBT, single, and transient people. Residents of public housing were subject to (or were challenged to elude) the watchful and often discriminatory eye of the Chicago Housing Authority. We were fortunate

Figure 5. *Laying Bare Their Private Lives,* c. 1920, by John T. McCutcheon. CHM, gift of George Barr McCutcheon II, ICHi-62275.

to engage the National Public Housing Museum as a partner in this collecting project. One way we display this complicated story is to include oral histories from LGBT and same-sex families in housing projects.

The second section is also organized around dynamics of inclusion—being welcomed inside a home—and exclusion—being rejected, being homeless, having no place to go. We were very interested in exploring structures of queer homes as places of refuge, where friends open their doors to anyone in need, thereby forming and embracing families of choice. Chicago House and Social Service Agency, one of the oldest AIDS service organizations in the city, provided a home for homeless people diagnosed with HIV and AIDS. In sharp contrast, the ongoing plight of homeless LGBTQ youth in Chicago is represented through a collaboration with About Face Theatre's Youth ensemble. We worked with the Chicago-based theatre company to incorporate their "Home Project" performance, a play based on numerous interviews with homeless teens across the city. Our visitor-panel group did not request, but rather demanded, that we acknowledge this urgent issue in the exhibition.

Section 3: In the Life

For many Chicagoans and members of the LGBT community, the stories and themes explored in section three represent much of what they know, appreciate, and expect of LGBT history. We entered into planning this section aware of the many fun and exciting stories awaiting us in the bars and bathhouses across the city, but were also challenged to offer a fresh interpretation on often-told tales of communities and places whose function go deeper than providing means for playful or sexy diversions. We wanted to talk about these social spaces as spaces with serious political consequences.

"In the Life" takes visitors beyond the walls of the home to explore the social worlds LGBT people have created in the public sphere. We examine the contested nature of space, in terms of its ability to bring people together and simultaneously produce exclusions, as well as the role that the police played in forcibly controlling the illicit. In this section, we argue that Chicago's history as a city of neighborhoods, nightlife, and bars, all of which were often segregated by race and class, had an effect on how LGBT people crafted community spaces and experiences that bridged the "private" world of the home and the traditional political sphere. Ultimately, this section suggests that spaces that appeared to be benignly about recreation, whether in the form of drinking, dancing, or even reading, held profoundly political meanings that shaped the course of LGBT struggles against homophobia and for equality.

It became apparent during our research and reinforced by feedback from our visitor panels that bars spanning the city, from Bronzeville on the South Side to the Bughouse Square on the North Side, should anchor our story. Bronzeville, in particular, had to be here because in the early twentieth century it hosted a range of spaces where a multiracial queer life was both visible and flourishing (fig. 6). There we found bisexual women like Ma Rainey and male-loving men like Tony Jackson minced no words when expressing the realities of sex, longing, and rejection in song, and where world's fair icon Sally Rand inspired drag fan-dances at the Cabin Inn, one of the most popular (and queerest) black cabarets of the 1930s. A section on cruising spaces highlights different kinds of sexualities and cultures, anchored by a mural from the original Gold Coast leather bar on North Clark Street in the Towertown neighborhood (fig. 7). This subsection also looks at how open and public spaces like the lakeshore provided space for gay encounters or lesbian gatherings, while privileged spaces such as the Chicago Athletic Association were known for coded and cloaked opportunities for gay sex.

Our challenge was to create a context for bars that expressed their many functions beyond sites of sexual encounters and drinking. Bars reveal tensions in and differences between LGBT communities, particularly in terms of race and gender. Perhaps because of this, LGBT bars became sites of study for social scientists who found ample ground to cover in Chicago. Beginning in the 1930s, scholars such as Ernest Burgess of the University of Chicago and Alfred Kinsey of Indiana University came to Chicago to study its queer bar culture. Their work revealed to outsiders unknown worlds representing a vast spectrum of sexuality across the city, and in many ways produced the archive that grounds *Out in Chicago*.

But we knew that bars and spaces for sex, even with our expansive interpretation of them, were not everything. We explore provocative subjects on politics, nonconformity, and sexuality discussed by Chicago's literati at the Dill Pickle Club on the North Side in the 1920s, and turn a few pages of torrid pulp novels at a corner drugstore on the West Side, where a library card was all it took to transport a curious reader into new worlds of sexual discovery. From Chicago, writers such as Henry Fuller and Margaret Anderson put forth powerful messages about politics, sexuality, and love (fig. 8). Decades later, university students and activist groups printed

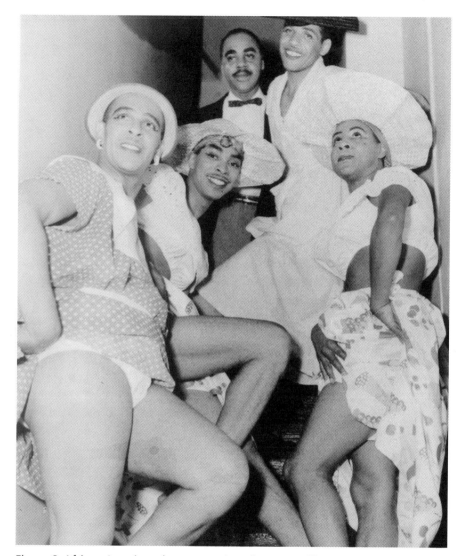

Figure 6. African American drag entertainers in Bronzeville. CHM, gift of Scotty Piper, ICHi-24648.

Figure 7. Mural in four panels from the Gold Coast leather bar by Etienne
(Dom Orejudos), 1973. CHM, gift of Allen Schuh, 2007.

invitations for potluck dinners and controversial queer dances, relying on the printed word and physical distribution to communicate community to those in search of it. LGBT Chicago would not be the same without its beloved sports organizations, especially its sixteen-inch-softball leagues. The 2006 Gay Games brought LGBT sports and creative communities out in all their glory at Soldier Field, one of the largest public LGBT events in the city's history. Religious institutions, too, play a critical role in the lives of LGBT Chicagoans. We display the dense and tightly knit religious congregations of multiple faiths to show the potential sensuousness of spirituality. These are but a few types of communities that served as havens for social support, whether to meet life partners or to revel in the closeness of same-sex space.

Two essays featured in this book, one from the museum vault, the other more contemporary, contribute to the themes of community building and evolving racial segregation of community spaces in this section of the exhibition. First, we have published an incredibly influential 1983 essay by late historian Gregory A. Sprague (1951–87), whose collection represents the core—the heart and soul perhaps—of CHM's holdings on LGBT history in Chicago. We are pleased to reprint here the excerpt that appeared in *The Advocate*, we are honored

Figure 8. Writer Margaret Anderson and Jane Heap, c. 1920.
Courtesy of the University of Delaware Library.

to have been granted the opportunity to publish Sprague's essay and that he is posthumously present in this project. E. Patrick Johnson has updated the essay from his popular *Out at CHM* program on "Gays and Gospel," a lecture that synthesized the history of African American music, religion, and oral history to make a case for queerness in African American communities of faith.

Section Four: Queers Mobilize Chicago

Something truly exciting happens when the one becomes the many in an urban environment like Chicago. Indeed, the energy that individuals create when mixing together to form a city, from early lawbreakers to today's genderqueer generation, is a theme that has remained a foremost interest for us throughout *Out in Chicago*. The final section is an extended discussion of how LGBT people became a political force for their own destiny in Chicago.

The city has both a rich and rocky place in American political history. It is a center of Democratic politics, whether in the form of the Daley machine(s) or the myriad activists who have fought back against the dominant politics by embracing protest and resisting the status quo. Not surprisingly, LGBT people have played an important role in this agitation, a subject that has been better documented by a range of scholars and writers than almost any other topic of substance in LGBT history.

We believed that most visitors, whether they have been exposed to LGBT history or not, would have an understanding of LGBT politics, so we wanted to go beyond the well known. How could we tell the story of Chicago LGBT politics in a new way? Our LGBT visitor panel insisted that we could not recount a narrative that implied unobstructed progress. They resisted a model where liberal inclusion meant that LGBT people were on their way to becoming integrated into mainstream society, whether through the securing of marriage rights or the ability to serve openly in the military. Instead of a model that pictured a unified LGBT community or political bloc, the visitor advisors wanted us to talk about how mainstream gay politics, with its interests in inclusion, often had exclusionary consequences. This was most clear in the case of how issues got on the "gay agenda" or put more simply, who defined what the most pressing issues facing gay people were. In particular, we heard real interest in a serious and extended discussion of how race and racism mattered in the historical evolution of LGBT politics. How had "white" come to be an invisible, yet defining, adjective preceding LGBT?

Given what we had to cover in this section, it quickly became clear that it was impossible to tell all the stories of political activism we needed to tell. We decided to focus on six vignettes, each of which highlight a different historical moment in LGBT politics and political activism in the city of Chicago, in an attempt to speak to how power-functions within and against LGBT agents of change. Using documentary-film–making techniques, we narrate six stories: the founding of the Society for Human Rights in 1924, the first organization committed to securing homosexual rights based in Chicago; lesbian attorney Pearl Hart's fight for the rights of marginalized people and the Chicago Police Department's Red Squad surveillance of her from 1939 until 1973; the radicalism of the LGBT movement in the 1960s and 1970s (fig. 9); the evolution of Latina lesbian activism in Chicago from the 1980s to present; how the early history of gay and lesbian health activism influenced the evolution of a response to AIDS in Chicago beginning in the 1980s and running through to this day; and the development of transgender activism in Chicago. In the cases of police surveillance of LGBT people and Latina lesbian activism, authors writing in this volume inspired us, most notably John D'Emilio's essay on police harassment and the co-authored essay by Larry La Fountain-Stokes, Ramón Rivera-Servera, and Lourdes Torres on the compelling history of Latina/o activism in Chicago.

The example of our reimagining of the formation of the Society for Human Rights suggests how we tried to retell stories that many visitors may have heard before. The short film moves beyond a focus on Henry Gerber, the German immigrant and postal service employee based in Chicago, considered to be the group's main figure. While telling Gerber's story, focusing particularly on how the Chicago police targeted Gerber as a homosexual, we also discuss the "poor people" who joined him on the founding board of the society. We describe the lives of Reverend John T. Graves, "a preacher who earned his room and board by preaching brotherly love to small groups of Negroes," and Al Meininger, "an indigent laundry queen" and bisexual with a wife and two children.[7] Graves was president of the Society for Human Rights, and the 1910 census recorded him as a single thirty-four-year-old black man from Virginia whose occupation was listed as minister at a church. While we know less about Meininger, both men's presence in founding documents suggest that the history of LGBT activism has long involved people of color and working-class people, not just white middle-class men. Graves's participation also raises important questions about what the Great Migration of African Americans meant for homophile activism in Chicago and beyond.

We wanted to make clear that Chicago's LGBT communities, politics, and identities are far from monolithic. At times this disparate group has coalesced around particular events, while at other moments we have seen Chicago's movement, if there is such a thing, fracture into many pieces. Ultimately this section tells the stories that hope to stand in for the thousands of LGBT people who have voiced their causes in the streets as well as others whose experiences have been silenced either by design or force. The last object in the gallery is a motorcycle belonging to Debby Rijos, the current leader of Chicago's chapter of Dykes on Bikes. From Chicago's West Side, Rijos assumed leadership of Dykes on Bikes in 2007 at the request of her aunt, founder Antonia "Tata" Flores. Following her aunt's legacy, Rijos sees riding as "a celebration of our pride and common cause together" (fig. 10).

Figure 9. *Lavender Woman,* CHM, ICHi-62295.

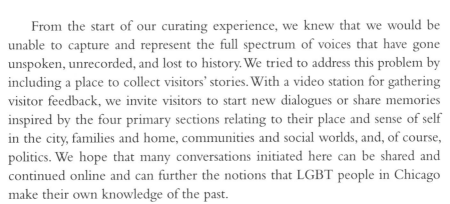

Figure 10. Debby Rijos at the 2010 Chicago Pride Parade. Courtesy of Debby Rijos.

From the start of our curating experience, we knew that we would be unable to capture and represent the full spectrum of voices that have gone unspoken, unrecorded, and lost to history. We tried to address this problem by including a place to collect visitors' stories. With a video station for gathering visitor feedback, we invite visitors to start new dialogues or share memories inspired by the four primary sections relating to their place and sense of self in the city, families and home, communities and social worlds, and, of course, politics. We hope that many conversations initiated here can be shared and continued online and can further the notions that LGBT people in Chicago make their own knowledge of the past.

We end this essay where we began it, in the galleries of the Chicago History Museum looking for LGBT history. We found ourselves in *Facing Freedom*, CHM's exhibition about the long arch of struggles for justice in American history. Recently, a group of Chicago high school students visited the Chicago History Museum, and staff interviewed them about what they thought were the most pressing civil rights issues of today. Teen after teen identified LGBT rights, and marriage rights in particular, as a central issue that should be included in an exhibition on civil rights (fig.11). We hope *Out in Chicago* is only one step on the path to LGBT history becoming a permanent part of the Chicago History Museum.

20

Gay Rights

Same sex marriage

The Question of should gay men & Women be allowed in the Army

If the U.S is a country where freedom is very important & everyone is equal then people that are GLBT should have the right/freedom to be happy about who they are w/out people making it a big deal. Its important because many people are scared to reveal their feelings because of the way people think of them.

Because people should have the freedom to pick their partners. love can never be wrong, gender doesn't matter.

I think that gay's should have the right to live their life how they want they shouldn't be juged. And they should have the right to abopt, get married, & go to the armmy

MANY PEOPLE FIND IT HARD TO Demonstrate THEIR sexuality IN PUBLIC. MANY People Dont know how to express it Due To THE Judgment OF THE PUBIC Due To behavior.

Everyone should be able to have same benefits as heterosexuals & should not judge by sexual preference

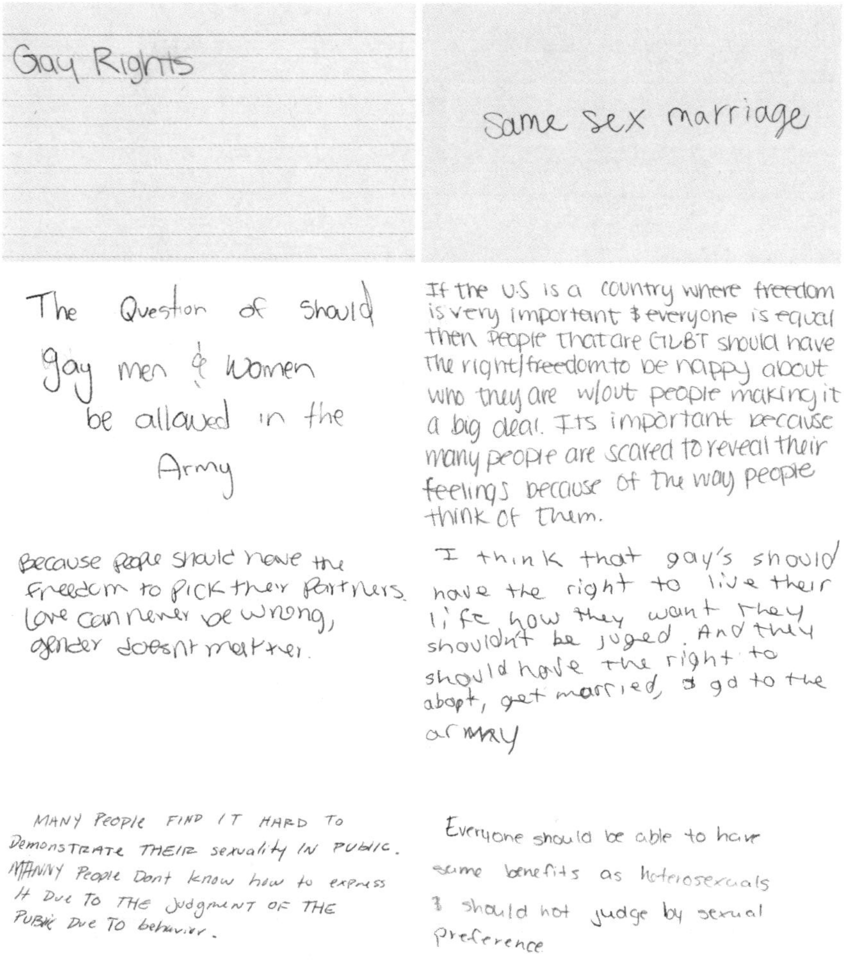

Figure 11. Examples of cards submitted by students to the Chicago History Museum.

ENDNOTES

1. We were inspired for both this essay and in the exhibition by Julie Abraham, *Metropolitan Lovers: The Homosexuality of Cities* (Minneapolis: University of Minnesota Press, 2009). We are also in debt to the handful of historians who have done work on LGBT Chicago. See Chad Heap, *Slumming: Sexual and Racial Encounters in Chicago's Nightlife, 1885-1940* (Chicago: University of Chicago Press, 2010); Kevin Mumford, *Interzones: Black/White Sex Districts in Chicago and New York* (New York: Columbia University Press, 1997); Allen Drexel, "Before Paris Burned: Race, Class, and Male Homosexuality on the Chicago South Side, 1935-1960" and David Johnson, "The Kids of Fairytown: Gay Male Culture on Chicago's Near North Side in the 1930s," in Brett Beemyn, ed., *Creating a Space for Ourselves: Lesbian, Gay and Bisexual Community Histories* (New York: Routledge, 1997). John D'Emilio has also published a number of historical essays on LGBT Chicago in *Windy City Times.* While section of these works focus on Chicago, there is still no monograph dedicated to the history of queer Chicago. A handful of dissertations have emerged in the 2000s that deal with LGBT Chicago. See Tim Stewart Winter, "Raids, Rights, and Rainbow Coalitions: Sexuality and Race in Chicago Politics, 1950-2000" (Ph.D. diss., University of Chicago, 2009); Tristan Cabello, "Queer Bronzeville: Race, Culture and the Making of Black Homosexuality in Chicago, 1920-1985" (Ph.D. diss., Northwestern University, in process); and Katie Batza, "Before AIDS: Gay and Lesbian Community Health in the 1970s," (Ph.D. diss., University of Illinois at Chicago, in process).

2. While not directly about the Great Migration or even immigration, John D'Emilio's groundbreaking essay "Capitalism and Gay Identity," argues that the growth of the city at the end of the nineteenth century made the formation and articulation of gay identity possible for the first time. This article and idea was a driving force behind the exhibition. See John D'Emilio, "Capitalism and Gay Identity," in Ann Barr Snitow, Christine Stansell, and Sharon Thompson, *Powers of Desire: The Politics of Sexuality* (New York: Monthly Review Press, 1983).

3. *Becoming Visible: The Legacy of Stonewall: An Exhibition on the History of New York's Lesbian and Gay Communities* (New York: New York Public Library, 1994); Stephanie Snyder, ed., *Out at the Library: Celebrating the James C. Hormel Gay & Lesbian Center* (San Francisco: San Francisco Public Library, 2005); Jonathan Ned Katz, "Outhistory," Center for Gay and Lesbian Studies, http://www.outhistory.org (accessed February 8, 2011). Tracy Baim, "Chicago Gay History," Prairie Avenue Productions, http://www.chicagogayhistory.com (accessed February 8, 2011); The History Project, "The History Project: Documenting GLBT Boston" (accessed February 8, 2011) and Twin Cities Oral History Project, *Queer Twin Cities* (Minneapolis: University of Minnesota Press, 2010). The Velvet Foundation is currently working to establish an LGBT Museum in Washington, D.C., and the GLBT Historical Society in San Francisco opened the GLBT History Museum in January 2011.

4. Galen Moon, interview by Gregory Sprague, August 25, 1980. Taped Interviews for the Gay and Lesbian History Project, Gregory Sprague Papers, Chicago History Museum.

5. The museum worked with an audience research firm, Slover Linnett Strategies, to conduct formative evaluation of the exhibition with members of Chicago's LGBT communities as well as people not connected to it, many of whom were members of CHM. The groups of twelve met three times over the course of six months to provide the exhibition team with detailed feedback about the themes and organization of the exhibition.

6. Our analysis on this section grew out of historian and *Out at CHM* contributor Susan Stryker, who clarifies "gender" (*being a man* or *being a woman*) as determined by cultural expectations, and outward appearances or physical shape, as opposed to the terms male and female, which correspond to biological or birth sex. See Susan Stryker, *Transgender History* (Berkeley: Seal Press, 2008) and "Screaming Queens and Lavender Panthers: A History of Transgender Activism," lecture delivered at the Chicago History Museum, May 8, 2008.

7. Henry Gerber, "The Society for Human Rights – 1925," *ONE* (September 1962): 7.

22

GENDER CROSSROADS
Representations of Gender Transgressions in Chicago's Press, 1850–1920

Jennifer Brier and Anne Parsons

Between 1850 and 1920, the *Chicago Tribune* reported literally hundreds of cases of gender crossing. Stories informed readers about female-bodied people who dressed and/or lived as men and male-bodied people who dressed and/or lived as women. The newspaper reported on some of this transgender behavior occurring in Chicago but also informed readers about similar incidents across the United States and in other parts of the world.[1] The news articles suggest that Chicago, like other turn-of-the-century cities such as San Francisco and New York, was a place where inhabitants could take on new identities and senses of self. While the particular details varied from article to article, in all but the shortest stories, there was a sense that the actions taken by transgender people were deliberate and often strategic.[2]

From the 1850s to the 1890s, accounts of gender crossing in Chicago almost always consisted of brief stories that focused on the exciting and illicit discovery and subsequent arrest of people dressed in the "wrong" clothes. The stories often took on an air of mystery, but rarely painted a detailed picture of the gender crosser. He or she existed as a trickster for the readership of the newspaper, and the stories suggested that neither reporters nor readers considered the lives of these gender transgressors worthy of column inches. The representations in the Chicago press began to change at the turn of the century, however, as the *Tribune's* brief reporting of arrests proliferated into in-depth articles about specific individuals who crossed genders. Reports after 1899 included incredible detail about transgender people, as well as intimate accounts of their everyday lives. In this respect, the newspapers seemingly began to produce popularized "case studies" that tried to explain the thinking and choices of individual transgender people. Curiously, none of these pseudo-scientific reports used the scientific language of the day, and they may have influenced the scientists more than historians have thought.

In this respect, the evolution of news coverage both reflected and potentially ignored the changing medical and social understandings of sexuality and gender in turn-of-the-twentieth-century America. While the late nineteenth century saw the development of a new science of sexuality and race, with Chicago serving as a central site for the evolution of this nascent field, the relationship between science and popular culture was far from unidirectional.[3] Home to the American Medical Association, the Chicago Medical Society, and the University of Chicago, the city was one of the main stops on a tour of early twentieth-century medicine in America. Nonetheless, Chicago-based medical professionals James Kiernan and G. Frank Lydston, sexologists who became interested in detailing the intimate lives of people who transgressed gender and sexual norms, found evidence for their efforts in both scientific and non-scientific sources. These sources ranged from their interactions with patients and the scientific community to articles about gender transgressors in Chicago newspapers.[4] While similarities in terms of the topic of gender crossing are found in media and scientific sources, the descriptive terminology varied greatly. Despite these potential disconnects, all of these sources were part of a larger system to control gender and sexual deviance in the rapidly changing industrial twentieth-century city.

Sexologists were not the only newspaper readers intent on learning about gender crossing. In this essay, we try to imagine what it might have been like for transgender people to find out about others like themselves through newspaper accounts. As Chicago newspaper circulations grew, and stories were being published regionally rather than merely locally, we know that tens of thousands of people read these accounts. Switching our historical perspective to center the experience of gender crossers allows us to suggest that both pre- and post-1900 newspapers served as a notification system of the penalties of gender violations and informed those people who crossed gender lines about arrests, court procedures, and how the accused responded to judges.[5]

We can make these arguments, in part because we relied almost exclusively on the *Chicago Tribune*, other national newspapers, and related government

24

documents. The *Tribune* was a self-proclaimed "businessman's newspaper" in the nineteenth century. With a circulation of between ten and thirty thousand readers in the 1870s and 1880s, it did not reach the mass audiences that the city's penny paper, the *Chicago Daily News*, did. But the *Tribune* published far more articles of local interest than the condensed *Daily News*, providing a wealth of stories about people who crossed gender boundaries. We read these stories cautiously, however. While the *Tribune* did not support government-sponsored welfare services, it did strongly support the city's police force, under the ideology that government should protect the interests of the individual.[6]

Our dependence on the *Tribune* raises many concerns for us as historians of gender and sexuality. While these documents provide invaluable historical details about how people lived their lives, when we study the history of transgender people through newspaper reports, court documents, marriage certificates, police photographs, and the like, we face the problem of who tells the story and how that narrator skews the lived experience of the person. In particular, we need to be cautious in recognizing that most of our examples are extant because the police made an arrest or the historical subject was under state surveillance.

Ultimately, the stories of nineteenth- and early–twentieth-century transgender people found in the pages of Chicago's newspapers speak directly to the larger history of Chicago. Instead of seeing Chicago as simply a physical crossroads where East met West in the emerging national railroad network and where immigrants arrived in huge numbers at the turn of the twentieth century, Chicago also became a metaphorical junction, where gender, geography, and politics intersected in powerful ways. Chicago transformed into a queer crossroads, where it was possible for people to exhibit a range of gender and sexual identities, even when they faced the power and opprobrium of the state.

Policing and Reporting Gender Outlaws in Early Chicago, 1850–90

Less than fifteen years after the incorporation of Chicago in 1837, the city's Common Council passed a spate of misdemeanor laws policing "offenses against public morals and decency."[7] Among the thirteen sections put in place in 1851 were ordinances regulating the mundane and the lascivious: regulations against swimming in the river, operating a tippling house on the Sabbath, and running a gaming house. That same year, the council passed regulations on animal and human sexuality, making it illegal to indecently expose a stud horse,

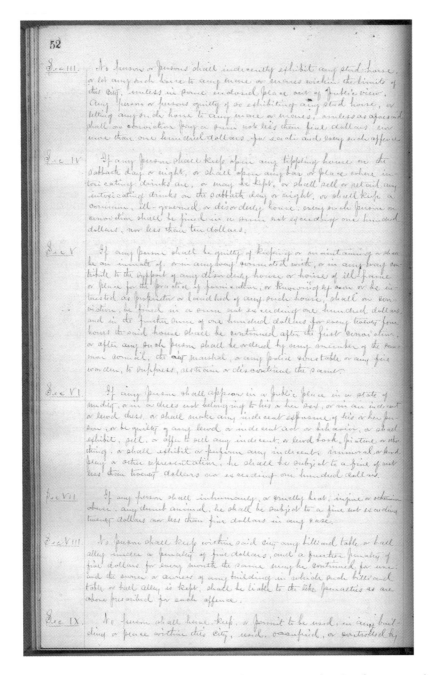

Figure 1. Reproduction of 1851 ordinance banning cross-dressing from Records of Ordinances by the City of Chicago Common Council. Courtesy of the Illinois State Archives.

allow a bitch in heat to run loose, or maintain or live in a house of ill fame.[8] Early Chicago politicians also regulated "lewd and indecent behavior" and punished people who appeared nude in public, exposed themselves, or solicited indecent books, pictures, and plays. Embedded among these rules was an ordinance that made it criminal for people "to appear in a dress not belonging to his or her sex, or in an indecent or lewd dress"[9] (fig. 1). While Chicago was not alone in outlawing cross-dressing, it was among the first cities in the United States to do so as part of broader morality campaigns against lewdness, vagrancy, disorderly conduct, and prostitution.[10]

The punishment laid out by the Common Council ordered that if someone were found in clothing of the opposite sex, the person should be "subject to a fine of not less than twenty dollars not exceeding one hundred dollars."[11] This amount was four times greater than the average five-dollar fine for law breaking in mid–nineteenth-century Chicago.[12] The fine was so stiff, in fact, that at least four male-bodied people petitioned the Common Council in the 1850s and 1860s to reimburse them for the fines they had paid.[13] Because Chicago's ordinance made cross-dressing a city misdemeanor, rather than a felony, the accused, in addition to paying a substantial fine, did not have access to the protections of indictment or trial by jury. This gave judges liberties when applying sentences to people charged as cross-dressers. Female-bodied people, as we will see in the examples that follow, often faced punishment even harsher than fines: they were regularly expelled from the city limits.

In the years immediately following passage of the ordinance, local constables and other law-enforcement officers unevenly applied the law and arrested and punished only some people caught crossing gender lines. Ordinary citizens and the press still policed gender norms, though, as in the case of Charley H., a female-bodied person arrested for being a man. In light-hearted prose, the *Tribune* in July 1857 opened an article by discussing the life of a young man named Charley, a hard-working clerk who lived in a boarding house and was a "something of a 'blood.'"[14] About halfway through the article, the *Tribune* revealed the surprise. While living at the boarding house, Charley had "determined to become acquainted with the lady boarders, and of course succeeded. Here was Charley's first great blunder. He ought to have known how much shrewder women are than men in detecting the real character of those they come in contact with."[15] Charley's acquaintances were "astonished to learn that Charley was a—woman, yes a veritable woman in man's apparel. This discovery was made on Monday evening and Charley, in her own proper garments—crinoline, and all, was on her way to St. Louis before midnight."[16] At no point in the article did the police appear, reflecting the lack of consistent state-sponsored action against gender crossing, even after the passage of an ordinance outlawing it. Whether Charley left the city because he knew about the stiff penalties he faced, we will never know. However, we do know that rather than stay around and face the court, Charley left the small burgeoning city of Chicago and made his way to the bigger metropolis of St. Louis.[17] He never again appeared in the pages of the *Tribune.*

The police played a more prominent role in the arrest of Harry/Mary Fitzallan five years later in April 1862. The *Tribune* opened the article with a description of a police officer patroling his beat. According to the newspaper, when he spied a female-bodied person in men's clothing, "Of course he arrested her, charging that she was a woman in man's attire."[18] The officer then took Fitzallan to court, where he testified that he was from Kentucky, had worn male habiliments, worked as a farm hand, and served as a Union soldier.[19] When the court questioned Fitzallan further, the article reported that "she refused to be communicative…. She stood in the presence of the Magistrate with not a bold but confident air, answered the few questions she wished to respond to deliberately, and apparently truthfully."[20] Rather than enforcing the fine, the judge suspended its execution if Fitzallan would leave the city. Refusing to change into female clothes, Fitzallan exited and walked down the street as a man. The *Tribune* closed the story by speculating, "Whether she will take her departure for Canada, or remain here, hunting up a friend—or lover— and again get arrested, remains for the future to solve."[21] Fitzallan was far from unique in this regard. At least nine instances of female-bodied people ordered to leave the city between 1851 and 1906 were reported in the *Tribune* alone.[22]

Some transgender people refused to be permanently exiled, however, and in the process found ways to resist the state's increasing surveillance. Just after the New Year in 1873, the *Tribune* reported on a female-bodied person dressed as a man who tried to come to Chicago via train. Alternately called "Miss Foster" and "Miss Annie M. Walker," he rode the Michigan Southern line into Chicago clad as a man when he was accused, by the train's conductor, of pickpocketing a fellow passenger. By the time the conductor filed a police report, Foster/Walker was ensconced in the city at a cheap hotel with his female traveling companion. The police tracked him down and arrested him for the theft. While being interrogated by police at the station, Foster/Walker aroused the suspicion of Superintendent Washburn, who questioned the suspect's "sex." Foster/Walker "stoutly" rejected Washburn's assessment that he was a woman, but Washburn persisted and "intimated that steps would be taken to establish her sex." This threat of bodily investigation by the state forced Foster/Walker to "own to her sex, and [give] her name." Foster/Walker then explained that he "donned male attire for the purposes of travelling to Chicago without molestation."[23]

The next day, the *Tribune* reported that Superintendent Washburn, after inviting Foster/Walker to dinner at his house the night of his arrest, planned to send Foster/Walker back to his hometown of Springfield, Massachusetts. While it is not clear why they dined together, there is some indication that it was part of the performance of concern about gender crossing. Not willing to trust that Foster/Walker would actually leave Chicago, Washburn arranged for him to be accompanied by a local detective on his way to visit family in Boston.[24] The return trip caused its own uproar, including a farcical report of the trip in the Pittsburgh *Gazette* where a reporter imagined that the two travelers made up a "May and December—An Eloping Pair from Chicago," even as Foster/Walker remained in his masculine garb.[25] The homoerotic nature of the account was not likely lost on readers and also probably suggested that the press saw this as a comedy in the process of unfolding.

The police were clearly not amused, however, when only a week later Foster/Walker returned to Chicago by train, this time dressed as a woman. "Determined to go West," the gender crosser, now named by the reporter as "Miss Annie M. Walker," announced that "she knew where she was going," even if the policeman who previously arrested her "did not." Foster/Walker's insouciance was felt even after her departure; Superintendant Washburn reported receiving a letter from Foster/Walker in which he thanked him for the return trip to Massachusetts and included riddles intended to annoy Washburn. The article reprinted the letter and ended with the claim that it was probably "spurious."[26]

What are we to make of these three stories of gender transgression in the budding city of Chicago? First, the state's failure to consistently apply punishment for cross-dressing between 1851 and the late 1870s suggests that during this period Chicago still had strong vestiges of its status as a frontier town and had not yet become the fully consolidated municipal power it would be by the turn of the century.[27] Even in the face of police action, transgender individuals had room to affect their circumstances, whether in the form of leaving town without supervision or refusing to stay away. In certain respects, for transgender people, the city's inchoate power structure meant they had some flexibility when "caught" cross-dressing. Prostitution, gambling, and other moral vices

29

perhaps attracted more attention in some instances because they offered police financial gain with bribes and payoffs. On the other hand, on a continuum of urban disorder, the police and courts may have viewed gambling and prostitution as more acceptable, and gender crossing as a potentially more serious threat to urban order.

Second, we can see the makings of a notification system in the emerging press of the period. Newspapers were central to the unfolding of these stories, particularly the case of Foster/Walker. In this case, with references to newspapers in Springfield, Pittsburgh, and Chicago (and potentially a claim that the whole story was manufactured by Foster/Walker in conjunction with reporters), clearly reporters saw stories of gender transgression as something that enticed readers and sold papers. With triple the readership, even if parts of the stories were falsified, the number of people exposed to the reports of gender transgression was significant. Newspapers such as the *Tribune* played a major role in securing order and shaping urban identity.

Third, it is possible to imagine that other people who defied contemporaneous gender norms read these stories of gender crossing and found important information in them. Stories of gender crossing inspired other female-bodied people in nineteenth-century America, as in the case of Sarah Emma Edmonds, a female-bodied person who lived as a girl, became a man to fight in the Civil War, and then returned to her life as a woman. While Edmonds did not have ties to Chicago, her story offers a glimpse into how some people learned to live across the gender line through the process of reading. Edmonds wrote a memoir of her experiences and discussed her life in an interview with a Kansas newspaper in 1884, during which she talked about what happened when she learned of a female-bodied person who dressed as a man. As a child, Edmonds received a book of fiction called *Fanny Campbell, the Female Pirate Captain*, published in 1846. In the book, the eponymous character's lover was taken prisoner in the Caribbean, and, in an attempt to save him, Fanny cut off her hair and dressed as a boy. Edmonds remembered that reading the book made her feel:

> as if an angel had touched me with a live coal from off the altar. All the latent energy of my nature was aroused, and each exploit of the heroine thrilled me to my finger tips. I went home that night with the problem of my life solved. I felt equal to any emergency. I was emancipated! And I could never again be a slave. When I read where Fanny cut off her

brown curls, and donned the blue jacket, and stepped into the freedom and glorious independence of her masculinity, I threw up my old straw hat and shouted. . . . The one drawback in my mind was this: She went to rescue an imprisoned lover, and I pitied her that she was only a poor love-sick girl, after all, like too many I had known, and I regretted that she had no higher ambition than running after a man. Perhaps later on in life, I had more charity, and gave her a credit mark for rescuing any-body — even a lover. . . . From that time forth I never ceased planning escape, although it was years before I accomplished it.[28]

The proliferation of stories in newspapers potentially served as a notification system of the policing and penalties for gender nonconformity and the tactics that arrested people used to avoid detection and plead their cases with the court. These stories also suggest that there was the potential for freedom in gender crossing, especially for female-bodied people. While none of the printed materials set out to inform transgender people about other transgender people, as the printed word became more readily available to a larger reading public, these sources had the potential of educating other gender crossers in Chicago, its surroundings, and across the country about what happened when their behaviors came under surveillance by the government.

Creating, Not Covering, the Case Study

By the end of the century, the notification system at work in the pages of the *Tribune* began to change. From the 1850s through the 1880s, many transgender people appeared only one time in the pages of the newspaper. By the 1890s, the media began printing serial stories about them and tracked gender crossers from city to city. On the surface these public dossiers mirrored the case studies written by contemporaneous sexologists, including Havelock Ellis, James Kiernan, and G. Frank Lydston. Beyond the veneer, however, newspaper report-ers never used the language of science—for example, Ellis's term *sexual invert*—to describe their gender-transgressing subjects.[29]

Instead, it seems that scientists looked to the newspaper for material that they could transform into scientific case studies. The first of these serial stories focusing on gender and sexual transgression appeared in 1899, when the *Tribune* printed half a dozen articles on Ellis Glenn, a transgender person who worked as a sewing machine agent in the small town of Hillsboro, Illinois. Glenn was arrested for forgery, and, upon his incarceration, authorities discovered that he was a female-bodied person who presented as a man. Over the next several months, the *Chicago Tribune* reported on Glenn's trial and his subsequent run-ins with the authorities in West Virginia, Kentucky, and on his return to Illinois. Glenn's story introduced *Tribune* readers and Chicagoans to the "case study" of a gender crosser, but at no point did a reporter label him a sexual invert.[30] In fact he was not identified as a sexual invert until Ellis published a truncated version of Glenn's story based on the newspaper coverage in his revised *Studies in the Psychology of Sex, Volume 2* in 1915.[31]

In the last months of 1906, a few years after Glenn's story captivated *Tribune* readers, the paper once again reported on and actively created a gender-crossing drama in Chicago. The subject was transplanted Chicagoan Nicolai de Raylan, a clerk whom authorities discovered was a female-bodied person only upon his death that year. Over the next two years, Chicagoans were drawn in to a tale of "deception" that took them to Russia, New York, Chicago, Arizona, and back again. The *Tribune* presented de Raylan's story in painstaking detail and introduced readers to a medical "case study" of gender crossers.[32] De Raylan emigrated from Russia to America, where he eventually made his way to Chicago, a city of immigrants at the turn of the century. De Raylan lived in the city for over a decade and worked as a clerk in the Russian consul's office. He was married during most of his time in Chicago, first to Eugenia de Raylan and later to a woman named Anna Armstrong.[33] He struggled with illness, however, and, in the winter of 1906, traveled to Phoenix to soothe his pulmonary tuberculosis. De Raylan died on December 18, 1906, and an autopsy revealed that he was a biological female.[34]

As if this news were not worthy on its own, the *Chicago Tribune* chose to focus on Anna de Raylan's story as she tried to hold on to the inheritance she expected from her husband. Anna de Raylan vociferously challenged the claims that her ex-husband had female genitalia, because she feared the loss of her almost $8,000 inheritance if the courts deemed him female. As James Reddick, public administrator of de Raylan's estate, stated, "If he was a woman there was no relationship between these two and the estate goes to other heirs."[35] The *Tribune* reported that Mrs. de Raylan filed a petition with the court claiming that her husband's body was substituted with another. In response, the judge sent a small contingency from Chicago to Arizona to exhume the body.[36] Upon their return, the judge held a hearing, in which he heard oral testimonies of the witnesses that they had seen the disinterred naked body, recognized the body as de Raylan's, and confirmed the body as a woman's.[37]

The *Tribune* went well beyond reporting the narrative of the court case. In fifteen articles between 1906 and 1908, it compiled a case study of de Raylan, reporting on nearly every facet of his life.[38] The newspaper thoroughly investigated de Raylan's marriages and particularly researched how he had hidden his biological sex from his wives. In an article titled, "Wives Explain De Raylan Farce," a *Tribune* reporter interviewed two women, as well as a person who knew Anna de Raylan, in an attempt to expose the intimate details of de Raylan's life. The informants reported that de Raylan's son, about whom "so much discussion has arisen," was actually born to another man.[39] Another East Coast reporter tirelessly tracked down a woman who had boarded with the couple in Chicago. She openly described the sex life of de Raylan and his first wife to the journalist and claimed that de Raylan avoided having sex with his wife by flirting and going out with other women. She also stated that he refused to have sex with his wife in order to protect her from his consumption.[40] According to the boarder, Mrs. de Raylan confided that "she really had never been a wife to the man she loved."[41]

In addition to these investigations of how de Raylan deceived his wives, the findings of a young lawyer who had became infatuated with the story fed the *Tribune* reporting. Michael Feinberg, a twenty-year-old attorney who worked on the case against Anna de Raylan, acquired de Raylan's letters and diaries from his second wife. Even upon the completion of the probate case, in which the court deemed de Raylan's mother his inheritor, Feinberg still pursued the life of de Raylan. The *Tribune* published the article, "Diary Discloses De Raylan Plot," which described in detail his diary and personal letters. Covering the years 1888 to 1892, when de Raylan was in Russia and went by the name of Anna Taletsky, the *Tribune* reported the sordid details of de Raylan's alleged blackmailing of his own mother, his flight from the police, and his change to the opposite gender. The newspaper also detailed his romance with a young Russian woman, for whom he pined for years after leaving Russia for the United States.[42] The coverage of de Raylan's diary did not serve to humanize him but instead depicted him as a twisted person who manipulated his own mother and who remained obsessed with a teenager long gone.

This pathologizing impulse did not become concrete until sexologists took up de Raylan's story as evidence of the extent of sexual inversion in Chicago. De Raylan jumped from the pages of the *Tribune* into the pages of a major medical journal. In February 1907, the editors of the *Alienist and Neurologist*, a key journal in psychiatry at the time, wrote that this story of a "gynesiac man...

Figure 2. Anna Roseman, August 1915. CHM, Chicago Daily News negatives collection, DN-0065043.

Figure 3. Lillian Gates, 1909. CHM, Chicago Daily News negatives collection, DN-0007021.

has been lately puzzling the daily press, especially in Chicago."[43] Six years later de Raylan came under international scientific scrutiny when Havelock Ellis used his Chicago connections with James Kiernan and G. Frank Lydston to learn about the de Raylan case and published the case study in his *Studies in the Psychology of Sex, Vol. II.*[44] It was in these scientific works, not in the popular press, that gender transgression became a strictly medical phenomenon.

By the beginning of the twentieth century, Chicago was becoming a place where transgender people, the state, the press, and a burgeoning medical community consistently argued over definitions of gender as well as the status of those who transgressed gender boundaries. While this discourse often had violent undertones, the freedom made possible in the growing city of Chicago suggests that it was a crossroads where people were not always what they seemed. Some of the best evidence for this claim comes from two photographs found in the *Chicago Daily News* archive at the Chicago History Museum (figs. 2 and 3). The first image shows Anna Roseman, whom the police arrested wearing men's clothes in 1915. In the photograph, Roseman appears dressed as a woman and smiling at the camera. The second photograph shows Lillian Gates, whom the police also arrested for wearing men's clothing in 1909. Unlike Roseman, Gates remained in men's garb and refused to look at the camera. As the images make clear, Roseman's photograph and story appeared in the newspaper, while Gates's never saw the light of day.

We read this inclusion and exclusion, coupled with the subjects' radically different comportments, as evidence of the range of resistances to gender norms in Chicago. The photographs also show how the Chicago press, at various points in history, shaped the public's understanding of gender transgression, although it was never the only source of information. The transgender people themselves and their representations embodied, literally and figuratively, how the city became a crossroads and at the same time a critical queer space.

ENDNOTES

1. A three-part note on language. As is true with much of transgender history and theory, we had to make a decision about how to refer to our historical subjects. First, we use the terms *female-bodied person* and *male-bodied person* to refer to individuals who altered their biologically defined gender with the use of clothing, body alterations, and external markings. Second, we have decided to use the gender specific pronouns that accrue to the subject's outward, and chosen,

appearance instead of s/he. Finally, none of our subjects identified themselves as transgender, a term that came into use in the late twentieth century. However, because they explicitly crossed gender boundaries, we use the word "transgender" to describe these actions. Here, we follow historian Susan Stryker, who argues that transgender should be used to denote "the movement across a socially imposed boundary away from an unchosen starting place" (Susan Stryker, *Transgender History* [Berkeley, CA: Seal Press, 2008], 1). For a discussion on the evolution of language in the writing of transgender history, see also Nan Alamilla Boyd, "Bodies in Motion: Lesbian and Transsexual Histories," in *A Queer World: The Center for Gay and Lesbian Studies Reader,* ed. Martin Duberman (New York: NYU Press, 1997), 137–38. For an example of how a scholar changed his approach to talking about gender crossers, see Jonathan Ned Katz's revision of his 1976 pictorial essay on passing women. In his 2008 text, Katz openly discusses how the passing women section had become a historical artifact in and of itself, reflecting a time before transgender studies when people were read as homosexuals rather than transgender. (Jonathan Ned Katz, "Gender Crossing Women, 1782–1920," at http://outhistory.org/wiki/Gender-Crossing_Women%2C_1782-1920 [accessed September 12, 2010]).

2. For discussions of the media circulation of stories about gender and sexual deviance, see George Chauncey, "From Sexual Inversion to Homosexuality: The Changing Medical Conceptualization of Female 'Deviance,'" in *Passion and Power: Sexuality in History*, ed. Kathy Peiss and Christina Simmons (Philadelphia: Temple University Press, 1989), 87–117; Lisa Duggan, *Sapphic Slashers: Sex, Violence, and American Modernity* (Durham: Duke University Press, 2000); Joanne Meyerowitz, "Sex Change and the Popular Press: Historical Notes on Transsexuality in the United States, 1930–1955" in *GLQ* 4, no. 2 (1998): 159–87; and Clare Sears, "A Tremendous Sensation: Cross-Dressing in the 19th-Century San Francisco Press," in *News and Sexuality: Media Portraits of Diversity*, ed. Laura Castañeda and Shannon Campbell (Thousand Oaks, CA: Sage Publications, Inc., 2005).

3. Jennifer Terry, *An American Obsession: Science, Medicine and Homosexuality in Modern Society* (Chicago: University of Chicago Press, 1999); Siobhan B. Somerville, *Queering the Color Line: Race and the Invention of Homosexuality in American Culture* (Durham: Duke University Press, 2000), 15–38.

4. For a discussion of Kiernan and Lydston, see Jay Hatheway, *The Gilded Age Construction of Modern American Homophobia* (New York: Palgrave MacMillan, 2003).

5. This claim bears similarity to Meyerowitz's findings about the tremendous response from readers to the popular media coverage of Christine Jorgensen in the mid-twentieth century. See Meyerowitz, "Sex Change and the Popular Press," 175–79. We also rely on a growing body of interdisciplinary literature that suggests the need to resist assigning fixed meanings to the lived experience of gender crossers. In addition to the material already cited, see David Valentine, *Imagining Transgender: An Ethnography of a Category* (Durham, N.C.: Duke University Press, 2007).

6. David Paul Nord, "The Public Community: The Urbanization of Journalism in Chicago," *Journal of Urban History* 11, no. 4 (1985): 422–24; Nord, "Read All about It," *Chicago History* 31, no. 1 (2002): 46.

7. City Council of Chicago, Records of Ordinances Vol. 2 7/0030/01, Illinois Regional Archives Depository, Northeastern Illinois University, 51–53.

8. Ibid.

9. Ibid, 52.

10. Legal historian William Eskridge Jr. has argued that such regulation of cross-dressing was twofold. First, it was an attempt to control gender fraud, in which a person changed genders to commit a crime. Second, the nineteenth-century policing of cross-dressing was also a regulation of desire and became a precedent for later connections between gender nonconformity and sexual deviance. More recently, historian Clare Sears has suggested that San Francisco's 1863 law against cross-dressing was part of a larger spate of ordinances that attempted to exclude people with "non-normative bodies" such as Chinese immigrants, prostitutes, and the disabled, from the public space. See William N. Eskridge Jr., *Gaylaw: Challenging the Apartheid of the Closet* (Cambridge, Mass.: Harvard University Press, 1999), 27; Clare Sears, "Electric Brilliancy: Cross-Dressing Law and Freak Show Displays in Nineteenth-Century San Francisco," *WSQ* (Fall/Winter 2008): 170–87.

11. City Council of Chicago, "Record of Ordinances," 52.

12. Sam Mitrani, "Order in the Metropolis: The Origin of the Chicago Police Department, 1850-1890," Ph.D. Dissertation (Chicago: University of Illinois at Chicago, 2009), 30.

13. "Petition of William Slate and Frederick Camp," August 21, 1854, File 0755A; "Petition of John Shoch," March 12, 1855, File 1858A; and, "Petition of Peter Roher," June 18, 1866, File 0096A, City of Chicago Common Council Records, Illinois Regional Archives Depository, Northeastern Illinois University.

14. "A Female in Disguise," *Chicago Daily Tribune*, July 29, 1857: 4.

15. Ibid.

16. Ibid.

17. St. Louis was in fact a larger city than Chicago in the mid-nineteenth century, although Chicago would surpass it by 1880. James Neal Primm, *Lion of the Valley: St. Louis, Missouri 1764–1980* (St. Louis: Missouri Historical Society Press, 1998), 3rd ed. 222–24, 272.

18. "A Romantic Female," *Chicago Tribune*, April 18, 1862: 4.

19. Ibid.

20. Ibid.

21. Ibid.

22. For examples, see "A Female in Disguise," *Chicago Daily Tribune*, July 29, 1857: 1; "The Feminine in Male Apparel," *Chicago Press and Tribune*, January 21, 1860: 1; "A Female Soldier," *Chicago Tribune*, December 18, 1862: 4; "The City," *Chicago Tribune*, September 17, 1864: 4; "Simonds and Son: How a Pittsburgh Reporter Manufactured a Sensation," *Chicago Daily Tribune*, January 19, 1873: 4. Jonny

Hoyt, a.k.a. Kate Parker, also left Chicago after his arrest: "A Woman in Male Attire," *Chicago Tribune*, July 3, 1864: 4.

23. "On Her Travels," *Chicago Daily Tribune*, January 11, 1873: 5.

24. "The City in Brief," *Chicago Daily Tribune*, January 12, 1873: 3.

25. "Simonds and Son: How a Pittsburgh Reporter Manufactured a Sensation," *Chicago Daily Tribune*, January 19, 1873: 4.

26. "Determined to Go West," *Chicago Daily Tribune*, January 26, 1873: 1.

27. The literature on the subject of Chicago's consolidation is too vast to cite here. We began with William Cronon, *Nature's Metropolis: Chicago and the Great West* (New York: Norton, 1991).

28. Quotation is from an interview published in the *Fort Scott Monitor*, January 27, 1884, as quoted in Laura Leedy Gansler, *The Mysterious Private Thompson: The Double Life of Sarah Emma Edmonds, Civil War Soldier* (New York: Free Press, 2005), 5–6. For Edmonds' autobiographical account see, Sarah Emma Edmonds, *Memoirs of a Soldier, Nurse, and Spy: A Woman's Adventure in the Union Army* (DeKalb, Ill.: Northern Illinois University Press, 1999).

29. Havelock Ellis, *Studies in the Psychology of Sex, Vol. II, Sexual Inversion* (Philadelphia: F.A. Davis Company, Publishers, 1915), 3rd edition, revised and enlarged.

30. "Prisoner Proves a Woman," *Chicago Daily Tribune*, November 26, 1899: 2; "Ellis Glenn Arrives in West Virginia," *Chicago Daily Tribune*, December 14, 1899: 7; and "Glenn Case in Court Again," *Chicago Daily Tribune*, December 9, 1899: 3.

31. Ellis, *Studies in the Psychology of Sex, Vol. II, Sexual Inversion*, 247.

32. Here, de Raylan's case was similar to the exhaustive *Tribune* coverage of the Oscar Wilde and Alice Mitchell trials, a phenomenon discussed by Lisa Duggan in *Sapphic Slashers.*

33. *Eugenia Raylan vs. Nicolai Raylan,* De Raylan Divorce File, G 240095, Circuit Court of Cook County, Cook County Clerk of Court Archives. Marriage License of Mr. Nicolai de Raylan and Mrs. Anna Armstrong, Cook County Clerk of Court Archives; "'Wives' Explain De Raylan Farce," *Chicago Daily Tribune*, December 24, 1906: 3.

34. Certificate of Death of Nicolai de Raylan, Arizona, accessed on www.FamilySearch.com on July 31, 2009.

35. "Solving a Mystery of Sex," *Chicago Daily Tribune*, May 24, 1907: 9.

36. De Raylan Probate Case, P2-8482, Cook County Clerk of Court Archives. "Solving a Mystery of Sex," *Chicago Daily Tribune*, May 24, 1907: 9.

37. "Testimony re. Proof of Sex," De Raylan Probate Case, P2-8482, Cook County Clerk of Court Archives.

38. The more in-depth articles about de Raylan's life include "De Raylan's Garb Her Least Trick," *Chicago Daily Tribune*, December 23, 1906: 5; "'Wives' Explain De Raylan Farce," *Chicago Daily Tribune*, December 24, 1906: 3; "New Story of De Raylan and His Chicago Wife," *Chicago Daily Tribune*, December 30, 1906: 2; "Diary Discloses De Raylan Plot," *Chicago Daily Tribune*, June 26, 1907: 7.

39. "'Wives' Explain De Raylan Farce," *Chicago Daily Tribune*, December 24, 1906: 3.

40. Ibid.

41. "New Story of De Raylan and His Chicago Wife," *Chicago Daily Tribune*, December 30, 1906: 7.
42. "Diary Discloses De Raylan Plot," *Chicago Daily Tribune*, June 26, 1907: 7; "'Wives' Explain De Raylan Farce," *Chicago Daily Tribune*, December 24, 1906: 3.
43. "Editorial," *The Alienist and Neurologist,* 28 (February 1907): 108.
44. Ellis, *Studies in the Psychology of Sex*, *Vol. II, Sexual Inversion*, 248. For another example of news coverage informing sexology, see James Kiernan's discussion of Ralph Kerwinieo in "Invert Marriages," *Urologic and Cutaneous Review* 18 (1914): 550–51. Kerwinieo's story also appeared in Ellis's *Studies in the Psychology of Sex, Vol. II*, 249.

WALT WHITMAN
Boy-friends and Politics

Jay Grossman

During his long life, which extended from virtually one end of the nineteenth century to the other, American poet Walt Whitman (1819–92) lived and wrote in the endless, sustaining company of other men. He built his life and work upon the foundation of these emotional, affectionate, and sexual bonds. These relationships are the central facts of Whitman's biography.

Consider, for example, the joint photographic portrait of Whitman seated and facing "his rebel soldier friend Pete Doyle" (as Whitman captioned in his own handwriting at the top of the image) (fig. 1). The photograph, probably from the late 1860s, is about as close to a marriage portrait of two men as would be possible to find in the nineteenth century, except that it seems even more intimate than the standard images of man and wife. Indeed, another image shows Whitman and Doyle in a more traditional "marriage" pose: Whitman is seated and Doyle stands beside him with his hand on Walt's shoulder (fig. 2). In this portrait, Walt seems to be at once the bride and the groom, since he is seated (as the man often is in nineteenth-century photographs of married couples), while he also looks adoringly, like a wife, at his "husband" Doyle. In the photograph in which both Whitman and Doyle are seated, however, it is as if the camera has intruded on an intimate moment and caught the two men unawares. It has captured not only the expressions on the men's faces, gazing at each other, but also Doyle's left arm touching Whitman's left leg, and hidden from view by it. This is not simply emotional intimacy, but physical intimacy as well.

We can get a sense of how unusual this photograph may have seemed to some of its nineteenth-century viewers by recalling the words of Whitman's closest friends when they saw it many years later. We know about this

41

Figure 1. Walt Whitman and Peter Doyle, taken in Washington, D.C. by M. P. Rice. Though Whitman has written the year 1865 in the caption above, it's likely this image dates from the late 1860s. Library of Congress.

conversation because Horace Traubel (one of Whitman's literary executors) took it upon himself to transcribe his daily conversations with Whitman from 1889 until the poet's death in 1892, eventually published as the nine-volume *With Walt Whitman in Camden* (surely among the longest "writer's last words" ever recorded). Traubel recalled being in the room when the seated photograph of Doyle and Whitman came into view, and he recorded the conversation that ensued on Wednesday, January 16, 1889:

> I picked up a picture from the box by the fire: a Washington picture: Whitman and Peter Doyle photoed together: a rather remarkable composition: Doyle with a sickly smile on his face: W. lovingly serene: the two looking at each other rather stagily, almost sheepishly. Whitman had written on this picture, at the top: "Washington D. C. 1865—Walt Whitman & his rebel soldier friend Pete Doyle." Whitman laughed heartily the instant I put my hands on it (I had seen it often before)—Harned [Thomas Harned, another of Whitman's executors] mimicked Doyle, Whitman retorting: "Never mind, the expression on my face atones for all that is lacking in his. What do I look like there? Is it seriosity?" Harned suggested: "Fondness, and Doyle should be a girl"—but Whitman shook his head, laughing again: "No—don't be too hard on it: that is my rebel friend, you know," &c. Then again: "Tom, you would like Pete—love him: and you, too, Horace: you especially, Horace—you and Pete would get to be great chums."[1]

43

Protecting Whitman's reputation from charges of "degeneracy," "inversion," and "pathology" (as homosexuality came to be called within the realms of medicine and law at the end of the nineteenth century) was a large part of the obligation that Whitman's literary executors took upon themselves after the poet's death, and, from this conversation, we can see that some of their efforts had already begun. Thomas Harned's explicit statement that "Doyle should be a girl" makes this anxiety perfectly clear: close physical ties and expressions of desire and affection between two men are appropriate and acceptable only when exhibited between members of the (so-called) "opposite" sex.

Nevertheless, sanctions against gay expression, which prompted Harned's discomfort, were not as consistently applied in the closing decades of the nineteenth century as we might at first expect. In 1881, for instance, Boston's district attorney informed Whitman and his publisher about a number of passages that, he insisted, needed to be excised from the latest edition of *Leaves of Grass* on the grounds of obscenity. (Incidents like this helped establish the well-worn epithet "Banned in Boston.") It is worth noting that Whitman refused to make any of the cuts: "The list whole & several is rejected by me, and will not be thought of under any circumstances."[2] The incident is important not only because of Whitman's unyielding defense of First Amendment principles, but also because, in his list of passages to be excised from the volume, the D.A. entirely ignored any lines or sections from the homoerotic "Calamus" poems, marking instead only passages that depict explicit cross-sex sexual activity and especially poems with active and openly articulated female erotic desire. We are used to thinking about the Victorian era as one of extensive censorship and prohibition around all things sexual, but in this Boston D.A.'s opinion, at least, the depictions of relations between men in Whitman's poetry hardly raised an eyebrow, though Oscar Wilde's London conviction a few years later, in 1895, on charges of "gross indecency" reminds us how quickly some of these social prohibitions can shift, and with what tragic consequences.

In the pages that follow I aim to demonstrate Whitman's unequivocal, life-long romantic and sexual attraction to men, the traces of which can be found everywhere in his writings, while at the same time making another, perhaps more controversial claim: that Walt Whitman was not a homosexual. Although he wrote as passionately and insistently about the emotional, personal, erotic and—not least—*political* significance of same-sex love as any author up to his time, I argue that something precious in our collective histories and inheritance as LGBT people living in the twenty-first century is lost if we too hastily find in Whitman only a familiar version of our own present-day selves. More than a century after his death, Whitman still provides us with an opportunity to think about not only our own claims for inclusion, but also about what the costs may be for acceding too precipitously to the normative or the status quo. "With the twirl of my tongue I encompass worlds and volumes of worlds,"[3] Whitman wrote, and he still challenges us to do the same.

Walt Whitman revolutionized modern poetry. Throwing off regular meter and busting out of formal, rhymed stanzas, Whitman wrote in long lines that extended from one side of the page to the other at a time when poetry was usually neatly confined to tidy stanzas surrounded by white space. Whitman also invented the poetic catalogue (fig. 3), one of his most democratic

Figure 2. Peter Doyle and Walt Whitman, at the same session as figure 1.
William R. Perkins Library, Duke University, Trent Collection.

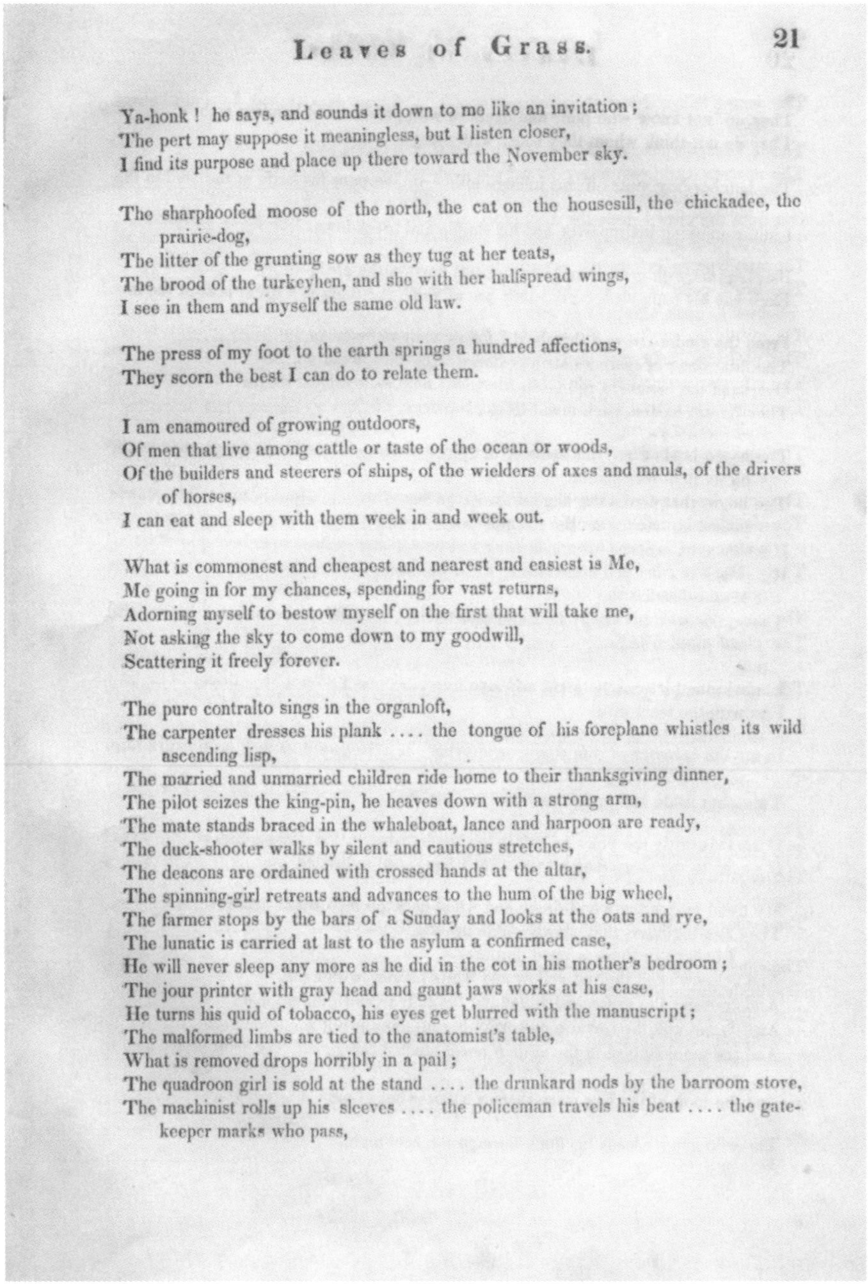

Leaves of Grass. 21

Ya-honk ! he says, and sounds it down to me like an invitation ;
The pert may suppose it meaningless, but I listen closer,
I find its purpose and place up there toward the November sky.

The sharphoofed moose of the north, the cat on the housesill, the chickadee, the
        prairie-dog,
The litter of the grunting sow as they tug at her teats,
The brood of the turkeyhen, and she with her halfspread wings,
I see in them and myself the same old law.

The press of my foot to the earth springs a hundred affections,
They scorn the best I can do to relate them.

I am enamoured of growing outdoors,
Of men that live among cattle or taste of the ocean or woods,
Of the builders and steerers of ships, of the wielders of axes and mauls, of the drivers
        of horses,
I can eat and sleep with them week in and week out.

What is commonest and cheapest and nearest and easiest is Me,
Me going in for my chances, spending for vast returns,
Adorning myself to bestow myself on the first that will take me,
Not asking the sky to come down to my goodwill,
Scattering it freely forever.

The pure contralto sings in the organloft,
The carpenter dresses his plank .... the tongue of his foreplane whistles its wild
        ascending lisp,
The married and unmarried children ride home to their thanksgiving dinner,
The pilot seizes the king-pin, he heaves down with a strong arm,
The mate stands braced in the whaleboat, lance and harpoon are ready,
The duck-shooter walks by silent and cautious stretches,
The deacons are ordained with crossed hands at the altar,
The spinning-girl retreats and advances to the hum of the big wheel,
The farmer stops by the bars of a Sunday and looks at the oats and rye,
The lunatic is carried at last to the asylum a confirmed case,
He will never sleep any more as he did in the cot in his mother's bedroom ;
The jour printer with gray head and gaunt jaws works at his case,
He turns his quid of tobacco, his eyes get blurred with the manuscript ;
The malformed limbs are tied to the anatomist's table,
What is removed drops horribly in a pail ;
The quadroon girl is sold at the stand .... the drunkard nods by the barroom stove,
The machinist rolls up his sleeves .... the policeman travels his beat .... the gate-
        keeper marks who pass,

46

Figure 3. Page 21 from Whitman's first edition of *Leaves of Grass,* showing the
start of his first "poetic catalogue": "The pure contralto sings in the organ loft . . ."

22   L e a v e s   o f   G r a s s.

The young fellow drives the express-wagon . . . . I love him though I do not know
    him;
The half-breed straps on his light boots to compete in the race,
The western turkey-shooting draws old and young . . . . some lean on their rifles,
    some sit on logs,
Out from the crowd steps the marksman and takes his position and levels his piece;
The groups of newly-come immigrants cover the wharf or levee,
The woollypates hoe in the sugarfield, the overseer views them from his saddle;
The bugle calls in the ballroom, the gentlemen run for their partners, the dancers
    bow to each other;
The youth lies awake in the cedar-roofed garret and harks to the musical rain,
The Wolverine sets traps on the creek that helps fill the Huron,
The reformer ascends the platform, he spouts with his mouth and nose,
The company returns from its excursion, the darkey brings up the rear and bears the
    well-riddled target,
The squaw wrapt in her yellow-hemmed cloth is offering moccasins and beadbags for
    sale,
The connoisseur peers along the exhibition-gallery with halfshut eyes bent sideways,
The deckhands make fast the steamboat, the plank is thrown for the shoregoing
    passengers,
The young sister holds out the skein, the elder sister winds it off in a ball and stops
    now and then for the knots,
The one-year wife is recovering and happy, a week ago she bore her first child,
The cleanhaired Yankee girl works with her sewing-machine or in the factory or
    mill,
The nine months' gone is in the parturition chamber, her faintness and pains are ad-
    vancing;
The pavingman leans on his twohanded rammer — the reporter's lead flies swiftly
    over the notebook — the signpainter is lettering with red and gold,
The canal-boy trots on the towpath — the bookkeeper counts at his desk — the
    shoemaker waxes his thread,
The conductor beats time for the band and all the performers follow him,
The child is baptised — the convert is making the first professions,
The regatta is spread on the bay . . . . how the white sails sparkle!
The drover watches his drove, he sings out to them that would stray,
The pedlar sweats with his pack on his back — the purchaser higgles about the odd
    cent,
The camera and plate are prepared, the lady must sit for her daguerreotype,
The bride unrumples her white dress, the minutehand of the clock moves slowly,
The opium eater reclines with rigid head and just-opened lips,
The prostitute draggles her shawl, her bonnet bobs on her tipsy and pimpled neck,
The crowd laugh at her blackguard oaths, the men jeer and wink to each other,
(Miserable! I do not laugh at your oaths nor jeer you,)
The President holds a cabinet council, he is surrounded by the great secretaries,

47

Figure 4. At the bottom of this page, the catalogue reaches the juxtaposition of
President and prostitute. When the catalogue finally ends halfway down the next
page, it concludes with a statement of shared democratic identity: "And such as it
is to be of these more or less I am."

innovations, a formal structure that he used to represent the democratic masses burgeoning everywhere around him in the city and nation. We can think about these long poetic catalogs as a mode of democratic inclusivity—though in political terms, of course, the women, African Americans, immigrants, Native Americans, and workers whom Whitman includes will have to wait to enjoy fully the nation's promise of equal rights and full citizenship. But that is also the genius of Whitman's poetic lines, which give equal weight and significance to each member of his poetic republic, as the speaker turns his full, line-long attention from "the pure contralto" to "the carpenter" to "the quadroon girl" to "the squaw" to the "cleanhaired Yankee girl," one after another, and one at a time, until a famous juxtaposition is reached at the bottom of page 22 (fig. 4):

> The prostitute draggles her shawl, her bonnet bobs on her tipsy and
> pimpled neck,
> The crowd laugh at her blackguard oaths, the men jeer and wink to
> each other,
> (Miserable! I do not laugh at your oaths nor jeer you,)
> The President holds a cabinet council, he is surrounded by the great
> secretaries . . . . [4]

Placing the prostitute next to the President, these lines exemplify the radical democratic impulse behind Whitman's poetic vision, as well as his full-frontal assault on polite literary values and bourgeois niceties. As he insisted in his 1856 letter to Ralph Waldo Emerson: "I say that the body of a man or woman, the main matter, is so far quite unexpressed in poems; but that the body is to be expressed, and sex is."[5] Other lines from his first book of poems further clarify his self-proclaimed mission:

> Through me forbidden voices,
> Voices of sexes and lusts . . . . voices veiled, and I remove the veil,
> Voices indecent by me clarified and transfigured.
>
> I do not press my finger across my mouth,
> I keep as delicate around the bowels as around the head and heart,
> Copulation is no more rank to me than death is.[6]

From the start Whitman shifted the landscape of what is possible to express in poetic language. By restoring the sexual to pride of place—beside the President, and including the prostitutes—Whitman insists on the poetic value and validity of the sexual and embodied aspects of American experience not previously treated in verse, while also keeping American politics at the center. His is a poetics of broad, inclusive democratic participation and representation. Indeed, the first word of the first edition of *Leaves of Grass* in 1855 is "America."

In his notebooks, Whitman collected and catalogued men in the same way he assembled other representative Americans in his poetry. Consider, for example, two entries from a notebook Whitman first used in New York City and then took with him to Washington, D.C., in 1862, when he began his service as a nurse in Civil War hospitals. Through these notebooks we learn about the friends and acquaintances with whom Whitman spent his nights and days (figs. 5 and 6).

> Peter Calhoun
> Oct. 10 '62   aged 26 23, born in Rome,
>   N.Y. worked in canal 3 years — his affair with the woman in
>   Brooklyn and N.Y. — my ride with him a trip and more at night
>   — 31 35 40 5th av
> has one brother younger, larger, works on the river — Pete told me of his
>   taking the $100 from home — also of David Helpers care
> of him when he had the bad disorder

> David Wilson — night of Oct. 11, '62, walking
> up from Middagh [Street]—slept with me—works
> in blacksmith shop in Navy Yard —lives
> in Hampden st. —walks together Sunday
> afternoon + night —is about 19

Loving, caring relations between men figure prominently in these notebooks: the first entry records how David Helpers took care of Pete Calhoun "when he had the bad disorder" (possibly syphilis), a story of compassionate relations between two men that Whitman records in his account of his own relation with Calhoun. The second entry also includes a detail Whitman is careful to specify in these notebooks, here and elsewhere (wherever possible!), that David Wilson "slept with me." While we can't know precisely what such "sleeping" entailed, it seems clear that this is a glimpse into a charged and

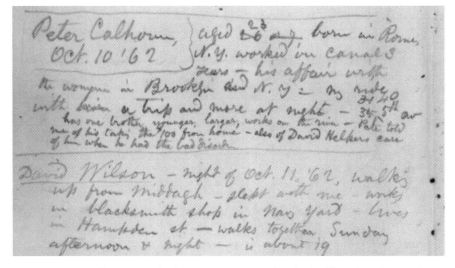

Figure 5. Entries from one of Whitman's 1862 notebooks, held at the Library of Congress as Notebook LC#94.

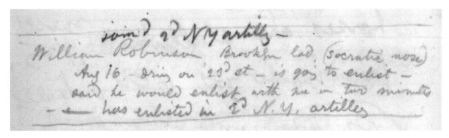

Figure 6. Another entry from the same Whitman notebook.

erotically explicit bond between men. Whitman records a similarly erotic moment with William Robinson, who, like Peter Doyle, was also a stage-coach driver in New York City:

> joined 2d NY artillery—
>> William Robinson Brooklyn lad (socratic nose)
>> Aug 16 — driving on 23^d st — is going to enlist —
>> said he would enlist with me in two minutes
>> — has enlisted in 2^d N.Y. artillery

In this example, enlisting in the army seems to serve as a kind of marriage proposal, the gist of which might be stated as: "I would love to have the chance to serve with you in the army." The entry also marks the near instantaneity ("in two minutes") of the bond that has materialized between Robinson and Whitman, who was frequently described by his contemporaries as possessing an almost electric ambience, attracting people of all kinds to him through his magnetic personality.

Peter Doyle's recollection of his first meeting with Whitman takes note of this same powerful presence:

> You ask where I first met him? It is a curious story. We felt to each other at once. I was a conductor. The night was very stormy. . . . Walt had his blanket—it was thrown round his shoulders—he seemed like an old sea-captain. He was the only passenger, it was a lonely night, so I thought I would go in and talk with him. Something in me made me do it and something in him drew me that way. He used to say there was something in me had the same effect on him. Anyway, I went into the car. We were familiar at once—I put my hand on his knee—we understood. He did not get out at the end of the trip—in fact went all the way back with me. . . . From that time on we were the biggest sort of friends.[7]

After Whitman's health deteriorated following a stroke in the early 1870s, and he moved to Camden, New Jersey, to be nearer to his family, Whitman and Doyle saw less of each other, though they remained in touch. But their separation did not mark the end of Whitman's romantic attachments to other, new boy-friends in the final decades of his life. On the contrary. In 1876, the poet met Harry Stafford, who was thirty-nine years his junior: "Dear Harry, not a day or night passes but I think of you . . . . Dear son, how I wish you could come in now, even

Figure 7. Bill Duckett and Whitman, photographed in Camden, New Jersey, in 1886, possibly by Lorenzo F. Fisler. Courtesy of Ohio Wesleyan University, Bayley Collection.

if but for an hour & take off your coat, & sit on my lap—."[8] As historian Jonathan Ned Katz has helped us to see, "Kinship terms—father-son, uncle-nephew, brother-brother—provided nineteenth-century males several ways to name and define intimacies between otherwise unrelated men and youths."[9] Whitman first became acquainted with Harry in a print shop where the 1876 U.S. centennial edition of *Leaves of Grass* was in production. Later, Whitman spent time with Harry at his family's White Horse Farm, near Kirkwood, New Jersey. He knew Harry's family, and years later, when Harry married and had a family of his own, they became acquainted with Whitman as well.

In the 1880s, Bill Duckett came into Whitman's life as his carriage driver in Camden, while also likely living at least part-time with the poet and his housekeeper, Mrs. Davis (fig. 7). "[Bill] was often with me: we went to Gloucester together: one trip was to New York: . . . we were quite thick then: thick," Whitman said.[10] And while it is a bit difficult to pinpoint the precise details of their relationship, Whitman and Duckett had at least one other thing in common: it is likely that they both posed nude for Philadelphia painter and photographer Thomas Eakins, himself a strong believer in the liberatory possibilities of the undraped human figure (fig. 8). Indeed, Eakins was fired as an instructor at the Pennsylvania Academy of Fine Arts when, as the story goes, he did not bat an eye when the draping slipped (or was deliberately pulled) from the body of a male nude during an anatomical sketching class that included women.[11]

Finally, at the end of Whitman's life, Warren Fritzinger came to live with Whitman to serve as a nurse during his last illness. "Warrie and I come to understand each other pretty well—*very* well. I like his touch and he is strong, a font of bodily power." A photograph taken at the Camden wharf in 1890 shows Fritzinger with Whitman (fig. 9). Warren was at Whitman's side when he died, and Whitman's last words seem to have been addressed to him, a request that Warren help him change positions in bed. ("Shift," Whitman said.) We might well imagine that each of these photographs of Whitman and the young men with whom he shared the last three decades of his life stand in for a wide range of unnamed others with whom Whitman shared his days and nights, and, undoubtedly, his love and his body as well.

Whitman's "Calamus" poems, which first appeared in the third edition of *Leaves of Grass*, are the poetic, published versions of the relationships with male friends

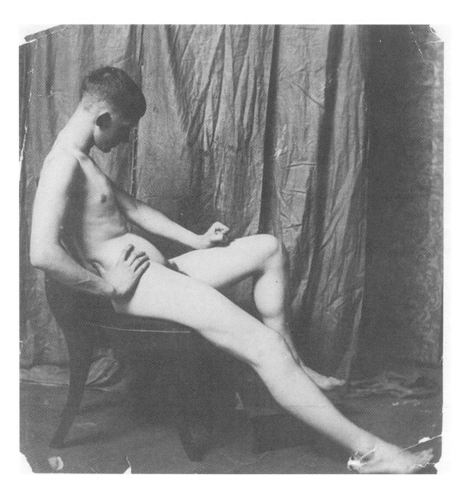

Figure 8. Bill Duckett, photographed by Thomas Eakins. Metropolitan Museum of Art, David Hunter McAlpin Fund, 1943.

Figure 9. Warren Fritzinger and Whitman, photographed at the Camden, New Jersey Wharf in 1890 by Dr. John Johnston. Library of Congress.

and lovers he recorded in his notebooks and photographs. Named for the phallic-looking marsh grass also known as "sweet flag," these poems make explicit the affectionate and sexual bonds between men that he placed at the center of his life. In "Calamus No. 11," for example, Whitman recalls a night like the one he shared with David Wilson:

> And when I thought how my dear friend, my lover, was on his way
>   coming, O then I was happy;
> O then each breath tasted sweeter—and all that day my food nourished
>   me more—And the beautiful day passed well,
> And the next came with equal joy—and with the next, at evening,
>   came my friend;
> And that night, while all was still, I heard the waters roll slowly contin-
>   ually up the shores,
> I heard the hissing rustle of the liquid and sands, as directed to me,
>   whispering, to congratulate me,
> For the one I love most lay sleeping by me under the same cover in the
>   cool night,
> In the stillness, in the autumn moonbeams, his face was inclined toward me,
> And his arm lay lightly around my breast—and that night I was happy.[12]

The speaker and his "lover" sleep together under the same blanket in mutual contentment. Elsewhere the "Calamus" cluster depicts not only occasions of intimacy between male couples, but also what we would recognize as cruising and the hustle and bustle of erotic anonymity that occurs in the city. Later Whitman renamed this poem "City of Orgies":

> City of my walks and joys!
> City whom that I have lived and sung there will one day make you
>   illustrious,
> Not the pageants of you—not your shifting tableaux, your spectacles,
>   repay me,
> Not the interminable rows of your houses—nor the ships at the wharves,
> Nor the processions in the streets, nor the bright windows, with goods
>   in them,
> Nor to converse with learned persons, or bear my share in the soiree or
>   feast;

Not those—but, as I pass, O Manhattan! your frequent and swift flash
    of eyes offering me love,
Offering me the response of my own—these repay me,
Lovers, continual lovers, only repay me.[13]

Here the poet luxuriates in the opportunities for masquerade, flirtation, and
spectacle provided by the urban crowd and the sweep of mass belonging, "one
of an average unending procession," as he elsewhere described it.[14]

Without a doubt, then, the "Calamus" poems—published, we should remember, on the cusp of the American Civil War—provide evidence of the explicitly
sexual and homoerotic Whitman that gay men and progressives of all stripes
have long celebrated. But they also demonstrate differences that are equally
crucial, and that underwrite my contention that Whitman was not a homosexual in the twenty-first century sense of the word. An extended excerpt from
"Calamus No. 5" brings these essential differences into view:

States!
Were you looking to be held together by the lawyers?
By an agreement on a paper? Or by arms?
. . . .
There shall from me be a new friendship—It shall be called after my
    name,
It shall circulate through The States, indifferent of place,
It shall twist and intertwist them through and around each other . . .
Affection shall solve every one of the problems of freedom . . . .
. . . .
One from Massachusetts shall be comrade to a Missourian,
One from Maine or Vermont, and a Carolinian and an Oregonese, shall
    be friends triune, more precious to each other than all the riches of
    the earth.
. . . .
It shall be customary in all directions, in the houses and streets, to see
    manly affection,
The departing brother or friend shall salute the remaining brother or
    friend with a kiss.
. . . .

The most dauntless and rude shall touch face to face lightly,
The dependence of Liberty shall be lovers,
The continuance of Equality shall be comrades.[15]

This prophetic poem imagines "a new friendship" as the basis for restoring unity at precisely the moment of national dissolution. Indeed, the poem puts its prophetic faith in "manly affection," which it also calls "Fraternity," in keeping with the French Revolution's trio of ideals alongside "Equality" and "Liberty." The poem strives to make the states newly "indissoluble" through the comradeship of lovers, and it prophesizes the ubiquity of visible affection between men: "It shall be customary in all directions . . . to see manly affection."

This poem also, crucially, extends the perimeters of male friendship beyond the bounds of the couple. Whitman explicitly writes about "friends triune," a sexual-political three-way between "One from Maine or Vermont, and a Carolinian and an Oregonese." A few years later Whitman reiterated the model in a letter to one of his "soldier-boys," Lewis K. Brown, during the war:

> You speak of being here in Washington again about the last of August—
> O Lewy, how glad I should be to see you, to have you with me—I have
> thought if it could be so that you, & one other person & myself could
> be where we could work & live together, & have each other's society, we
> three, I should like it so much—but it is probably a dream—[16]

Pushing the paradigm of the couple aside, Whitman shares with Lewy his ideal that a *ménage* rather than a simple pairing is where his heart alights when he fantasizes about their shared future. This, too, is an aspect of Whitman's difference from many, perhaps most, of his twenty-first-century heirs, for Whitman imagines a wider comradeship knitting together the nation and extending the reach of the sexual beyond the privacy of a couple living and loving apart. Here, in a word, is Whitman's queerness and his refusal to translate neatly into our categories. Instead, he stands apart from a role we might place him in, as, say, a forerunner of our own widely shared investments in gay marriage. We can have Whitman in this form (as a version of ourselves) if we want, but it will mean some "trimming around the edges," some cutting back on his own radicalism to fit our current-day political choices and comfort zone.

It is not only at the site of the couple that Whitman registers his difference from a great deal of contemporary LGBT politics. Another way in which we can mark the difference that inheres in Whitman's nineteenth-century "sexuality" is by focusing upon the explicit political purpose that he ascribes to these relations between men. Whitman's poetry directly and explicitly attaches his desire for men to its political consequences; he does not imagine relations between men as private, separate from the world, or isolated from the political. It would be unthinkable for him that "gays in the military" has come to seem, in some parts of dominant culture, an oxymoron or an impossibility. Indeed, two short poems about the "brotherhood of lovers" proclaim just the opposite:

> When I peruse the conquered fame of heroes, and the victories of
>   mighty generals, I do not envy the generals,
> Nor the President in his Presidency, nor the rich in his great house;
> But when I read of the brotherhood of lovers, how it was with them,
> How through life, through dangers, odium, unchanging, long and long,
> Through youth, and through middle and old age, how unfaltering, how
>   affectionate and faithful they were,
> Then I am pensive—I hastily put down the book, and walk away, filled
>   with the bitterest envy. [17]

> I dreamed in a dream, I saw a city invincible to the attacks of the
>   whole of the rest of the earth,
> I dreamed that was the new City of Friends,
> Nothing was greater there than the quality of robust love—it led the rest,
> It was seen every hour in the actions of the men of that city,
> And in all their looks and words.[18]

In its invincibility to "the attacks of the whole of the rest of the earth," in its "unchanging" and "unfaltering" persistence through "dangers" and "odium," Whitman's New Friendship is a force to be reckoned with, a stalwart crew able collectively to withstand all of the world's challenges. But these two poems ultimately place love between men, and not military force, at their center. Love is the real power here—"Nothing was greater there than the quality of robust love"—and the poems portray love and comradeship as both indomitable and pervasive. Whitman's "robust love" displaces the military, perhaps even the need for the military. Certainly, Whitman did not want us to put down *his* book "filled with the bitterest envy." But his work challenges us to keep in mind the political, real-world purport of "the quality of robust love" he depicted.

In the same way, Whitman articulated the opposite of the contemporary slogan "Keep the government out of my bedroom." Instead he advocated something like: "My bedroom and my cruising shall be the basis of government." Or: "The American city is my bedroom." "The strength of my Republic will be founded on the comradeship of men and lovers." For Whitman, sexuality was not the secret private core inside but rather a public principle, and he placed his sexual and affectionate attraction to men at the very center of his political plans and hopes for the nation. Recently the Gay Pride Parade in Chicago was kicked off by a vast assembly of LGBT parents and their children and families and allies, where once upon a time the legendary Dykes on Bikes were at the head of the pack. Someone else can decide whether this is a good thing or a bad thing. But Whitman helps us to see that it is a *different* thing, and that once upon a time the Gay and Lesbian Liberation Movement had more on its mind than gay marriage and military service. Thinking we know what a queer family looks like today may actually keep us from being able to see just how queer the notions of family, collectivity, and finally, politics, may have been for Whitman more than one hundred and fifty years ago.

In his 1870 essay "Democratic Vistas," Whitman wrote that "democracy infers such loving comradeship, as its most inevitable twin or counterpart, without which it will be incomplete, in vain, and incapable of perpetuating itself."[19] Insisting that "democracy infers . . . loving comradeship," Whitman pointed out the difference between his sexual-political universe and our own, even as he figured a kind of procreative potential in comradeship that, he proclaimed, is itself necessary for democracy to "perpetuate" itself. Now I would not be misunderstood: calling Whitman "gay" is a shorthand that *can* have genuinely positive political effects. Indeed, in the classroom, there may be few moments as powerful as when it is made clear that America's Poet of Democracy is also America's Gay Poet. But we should remember that it *is* shorthand, a simplification, and that this is a case where the word "queer" can also do some genuinely important work for us. There is something genuinely queer about Whitman and his boy-friends, comrades, and friends, something that *exceeds* the category of the homosexual as we use it today.

"Calamus No. 24" clarifies what is at stake in noting these distinctions between "us" and "him":

I hear it is charged against me that I sought to destroy institutions;
But really I am neither for nor against institutions,

(What indeed have I in common with them?—Or what with the
  destruction of them?)
Only I will establish in the Mannahatta, and in every city of These
  States, inland and seaboard,
And in the fields and woods, and above every keel little or large, that
  dents the water,
Without edifices, or rules, or trustees, or any argument,
The institution of the dear love of comrades.[20]

This poem reimagines the very concept of institutions, whether of the nation, or marriage, or the spoken and unspoken regulations of desire. Rather than, say, settling for a version of heterosexual marriage or civil unions, this poem challenges twenty-first-century LGBT people and their allies to dream bigger, to imagine a wholesale revaluation of the foundational structures of society. It challenges us to think outside the confining logics of "edifices, or rules, or trustees." Rethinking the possibilities of institutions, Whitman argued, will produce effects we've not even dreamed of. But what Whitman does not want is a retreat into some privatized zone apart—a space separate from history or government, from urban life or "forbidden voices." If we see him only as a poet of homosexuality separate from a transformative politics in the world, we will miss the radicalism that, for him, always travels alongside same-sex relations. Utopian it may be, but Whitman's America is the original Queer Nation.[21]

61

ENDNOTES

1. Horace Traubel, *With Walt Whitman in Camden*, vol. 3 (New York: Rowman and Littlefield, 1961), 542–43. I'm indebted to Ed Folsom's account of this conversation in his essay "Whitman's Calamus Photographs" in Betsy Erkkila and Jay Grossman, eds., *Breaking Bounds: Whitman & American Cultural Studies* (New York: Oxford University Press, 1996), 193–219.

2. Justin Kaplan, *Walt Whitman: A Life* (New York: Simon and Schuster, 1980), 20. Horace Traubel offers one of the earliest recountings of the Boston story: "Walt Whitman and His Boston Publishers II," *The Conservator* (Jan. 1896): 165.

3. Walt Whitman, *Leaves of Grass,* 1st ed., (Brooklyn, N.Y., 1855), 31. Facsimiles of all of the editions of *Leaves of Grass* are available online at The Walt Whitman Archive <http://www.whitmanarchive.org>.

4. Whitman, *Leaves of Grass,* 1st ed., 22.

5. Whitman published his famous open letter to Emerson in the second edition of *Leaves of Grass* (Brooklyn, N.Y., 1856), 346–58. This quotation appears on 356.

6. Whitman, *Leaves of Grass,* 1st ed., 29.

7. Richard M. Bucke, ed., *Calamus: A Series of Letters Written during the Years 1868–80 by Walt Whitman to a Young Friend (Peter Doyle)* (Boston: Laurens Maynard, 1897), 23.

8. Whitman to Harry Stafford, *The Correspondence,* ed. Edwin Haviland Miller, vol. 3 (New York: New York University Press, 1964), 86.

9. Jonathan Katz, *Love Stories: Sex between Men before Homosexuality* (Chicago: University of Chicago Press, 2001), 170.

10. Sculley Bradley, ed., *With Walt Whitman in Camden,* vol. 4 (Philadelphia: University of Pennsylvania Press, 1953), 65.

11. Many historians have told the story of Eakins's firing from the Pennsylvania Academy. See, for example, Sidney D. Kirkpatrick, *The Revenge of Thomas Eakins* (New Haven: Yale University Press, 2006), ch. 34; Elizabeth Johns, "Thomas Eakins and 'Pure Art' Education." *Archives of American Art Journal* 30:1–4 (1990): 71–76. Folsom discusses the nude photographs in "Whitman's Calamus Photographs," 210-17.

12. Whitman, "Calamus No. 11," *Leaves of Grass,* 3rd ed., (Boston: Thayer and Eldridge, 1860-61), 357–8.

13. Whitman, "Calamus No. 18," *Leaves of Grass,* 3rd ed., 363.

14. Whitman, *Leaves of Grass,* 1st ed., 43.

15. Whitman, "Calamus No. 5," *Leaves of Grass,* 3rd ed., 349–51.

16. Charley Shively, ed., *Drum Beats: Walt Whitman's Civil War Boy Lovers* (San Francisco: Gay Sunshine Press, 1989), 76.

17. Whitman, "Calamus No. 28," *Leaves of Grass,* 3rd ed., 370.

18. Whitman, "Calamus No. 34" *Leaves of Grass,* 3rd ed., 373.

19. Whitman, "Democratic Vistas" in *Whitman: Poetry and Prose,* ed. Justin Kaplan (New York: Library of America, 1996), 1,006 fn.

20. Whitman, "Calamus No. 24," *Leaves of Grass,* 3rd ed., 367–68.

21. I'm indebted for my conclusion to Henry Abelove's "From Thoreau to Queer Politics" in his *Deep Gossip* (Minneapolis: University of Minnesota Press, 2003), 40–41.

Queer or Not
What Jane Addams Teaches Us about Not Knowing

Victoria Bissell Brown

Author's note: I wrote and delivered this talk on Jane Addams at the Chicago History Museum in February 2005, a year after publishing my book The Education of Jane Addams, *which is about how Jane Addams became Jane Addams. At the time, I was both witness to and participant in professional debates over whether it was appropriate to discuss the sex life of a woman who was once referred to as "the only saint America has produced."[1] Those who argued that such talk was inappropriate relied on the fact that we have no certain proof of her sexual proclivities, while those who argued for discussion of Addams's sexuality implied that we know enough to presume the rest. When George Chauncey invited me to speak at the Chicago History Museum, he gave me a platform from which to voice my views on this debate.*

I know two things for sure: Jane Addams was queer. And Jane Addams would use one of her favorite words—"stupid"—to describe our discussion here tonight.

I am seldom visited by Jane Addams. Before my drive into Chicago today, she'd spoken to me just a few times in all our eighteen years together. But today she was in the car. "There are *how many* homeless children in Chicago these days?" she asked me. "How many teenage kids needing jobs and midnight basketball? How much is being spent every month in Iraq—a billion dollars, for heaven's sake? And you're driving to Chicago to talk about my *private* life?"

Mary Rozet Smith and Jane Addams, 1896. Courtesy of the Swarthmore College Peace Collection.

64

Questions about the legitimacy of my politics and priorities hung heavy in the car. Addams was quiet. She doesn't harangue; she haunts. Finally, I spoke. "Are you seriously going to argue that being queer, that knowing your life *had* to be different from other young women's, that aching for the freedom to live the life you wanted . . . are you seriously going to argue that your personal experience did not shape your politics? Did not give you empathy for the other? Did not give you affection for the outsider and make you want to embrace the misfit?" By the time the questions were out of my mouth, Addams had vanished. That's her style.

But I know Jane Addams was queer. I know she never once evinced the slightest romantic interest in a male, though she had opportunities. I know she never shared her schoolmates' assumptions of marriage to a picket-fenced future. I know she held her ground outside the orthodox circles of Christianity and heterosexuality. In my book on the first thirty-five years of her life, I state that Jane Addams "probably knew at seventeen that she was no more likely to take a husband in matrimony than to take Jesus Christ as her personal savior."[2]

I know that the most important person in Addams's emotional education was Ellen Gates Starr, that when the two women were in their teens and twenties, Starr taught Addams about sharing and trusting and confiding and committing. I know that when Starr told Jane her about longing for a departed female friend, she noted that other people could only understand "that kind of feeling" if its object "were a man."[3] I know that when Jane and Ellen were young and touring Europe together in 1888 but staying in different cities for one week, Ellen wrote to Jane of not sleeping well in the bed that was "even wider than ours," and wondered if she were "wicked to wish that you were on one edge [of the bed] and I in the middle comme toujours." I know that during that week apart, Ellen wished she could "excite and tempt" Jane by "kissing you fifteen times this minute."[4]

I know that the following year, Addams and Starr opened their settlement on Halsted Street and that Addams later wrote in her autobiography, "Probably no young matron every placed her own things in her own house with more pleasure than that with which we furnished Hull-House."[5] I know that Addams, whose family had money, did not financially support Starr, whose family had none. But early in their Hull-House venture, knowing that Starr was giving up her schoolteacher's wages to pursue their "scheme," Addams set aside a small fund for Starr in the event of Addams's death.[6] Sadly, I know that two years after these dear but temperamentally ill-suited friends opened Hull-House, Jane gave her heart and soul to Mary Rozet Smith, setting off an emotional earthquake in Starr's life that Addams chose to ignore. That, let's remember, was Addams's style.

But disengagement was not her only style. I know that four years after meeting Smith, Addams reminisced in a poem:

> One day I came into Hull House
> (No spirit whispered who was there)
> And in the kindergarten room
> There sat upon a childish chair
> A girl both tall and fair to see,
> (To look at her gives one a thrill).
> But all I thought was, would she be
> Best fitted to lead club or drill?
> You see, I had forgotten Love,
> And only thought of Hull House then.
> That is the way with women folks

When they attempt the things of men . . .
So I was blind and deaf
To all save one absorbing care
And did not guess what I now know—
Delivering love was sitting there.[7]

I know that Smith made Addams's life possible, emotionally and financially. Make no mistake here: Addams partnered well–and she knew it. Mary Smith's loving parents embraced Jane as their own daughter and put their vast financial resources in generous service to Hull-House. Smith herself took care of Addams, fussed over her, carried her shawl, handkerchief, and crackers; traveled with her; washed her hair; bought her clothes; buoyed her in health; tended her in illness.[8] In an undated poem that captures the queer space their intimately material lives occupied, Addams wrote:

The "mine" and "thine" of wedded folk
Is often quite confusing
And sometimes when they use the "ours"
It sounds almost amusing

But you and I may well defy
Both married folk and single
To do as well as we have done
The "mine" and "thine" to mingle.[9]

Clearly, Addams did not feel as economically dependent on Mary as women in traditional heterosexual marriages, but clearly, too, she did not view herself as a "single" person. Just as she innovated in social reform, Addams innovated in the intimate, domestic, and material arrangements in her life. However queer it may have been to "defy" convention as she and Mary did, Addams embraced that defiance and delighted in the spiritual and material support it brought her. For her part, over the course of four decades, Mary Smith devoted herself entirely to "making life easier for Jane Addams." According to Addams's nephew, James Linn, caring for Jane was Mary's "career, her philosophy."[10] A few months before she died, Smith thanked Addams for having "*made* my life. All its meaning and color come from you."[11] And at the time of Smith's death in 1934, just a year before Addams's own death, one mourning friend wrote that Jane was "the one through whom Mary found herself." Another friend wondered how Addams would survive the loss.[12] The answer was: she did not.

This comforting recital of what I *know* about Addams's queerness after eighteen years with her does not, of course, encompass what I do not know or what I think or what I think on most days.

I think that Addams should not be termed a lesbian. Queer, yes; gay, no. I take this political and historical position because the terms *lesbian* and *gay* are significant, conscious assertions of sexual behavior as central to social identity. They call up a sense of community cohesion based on a shared investment in same-sex eroticism, and I know that Jane Addams did not look to eroticism to define herself or her community.

If I chose to align with those who define a lesbian as a woman—any woman in any era—whose primary emotional relationships are with other women and chooses women to nurture and support in work and domestic life then, yes, I would define Addams as a lesbian.[13] But I cannot use a word that has purposely erotic meaning in our era to describe the intimate experience of a woman who lived in a very different time. Too many people have fought too hard for modern lesbians' claim to a lusty, erotic life for me to daintily retreat into an ahistorical definition of "lesbian" that skirts the blood, sweat, and tears of erotic expression.

Which begs the question: why do I pause before assuming an erotic identity for Addams? I have two reasons—one deriving from the evidence on Addams, another stemming from theoretical perspectives on the history of sexuality.

Just as the surviving letters from her youth make clear that the young Jane Addams never evinced the slightest interest in a romantic relationship with a male, they also make clear she actively disdained romantic ties to females. Just at the time of life when her classmates at Rockford Female Seminary were safely experimenting with romantic expression by indulging in sentimental schoolgirl "smashes," Addams stood just above it all, sharing a cousin's contempt for "the spooning malady" and publicly scolding her classmates for reading "enervating and foolish" love stories when they could be studying.[14] All around her, girls rehearsed for their heterosexual futures as wives and mothers, blending crushes on each other and crushes on the boys at Beloit College into a blur of desire, but Addams avoided it all. Though much admired, even beloved, as a leader among her classmates at Rockford in the years between 1877 and 1881, Addams spent her adolescent years resisting invitations to "descend," as she explained in a letter to Ellen, into the emotionalism of religiosity or romance.[15]

Having announced her preference for "cold people" and counseled her class-mates to discipline their affectionate impulses by making friends "of inanimate objects . . . unchangeable things," the young Jane Addams wrote private essays about an idealized female goddess whose "coldness and quiet" announced she "could be alone in the world and need no other support."[16] We can imagine multiple reasons for Addams's impulse to avoid emotional attachments, including her mother's death when Jane was two years old and her ambition to lead a public, not a private, life. The point here is that these impulses encouraged her to avoid the youthful explorations into romance and sexuality that characterized her class-mates' seminary days. Instead, she actively constructed a disembodied Mother Earth goddess as her ideal, responding to the corporeal reality of sex much as she responded to the spiritual demands of faith: with a bid for transcendence. "We can always think with a body or without one," the adolescent Addams insisted in one seminary essay, indicating in a letter to Starr that she thought of the soul as regret-tably "imprisoned" in "puny" and "perishable flesh."[17]

Was the young Addams fleeing her own emerging homosexual impulses? Perhaps. But she *was* fleeing them, not acting on them, even when Starr invited that action. For in no letter that Starr kept did Addams ever acknowledge Ellen's sexualized references. In response to her comment on "that kind of feeling," Addams said that humans can feel that way about *places* as well as people, and she forwarded Ellen's "15 kisses" letter on to her sister, Alice, with a cover note that blithely dismissed Starr's style of "demonstrative affection."[18] My reading of Starr's letters leaves me no doubt that she was in romantic love with Addams, and, given the chance, would have turned their shared bed into a site for more than warm affection. But Starr's love, like her religious and political tempera-ment, burned too hot for the cool Jane Addams. It was Starr's fate to be the person who pulled Addams out of her emotional shell in the eight years between Rockford Seminary and the opening of Hull-House, only to watch the maturing Addams realize her capacity for emotional attachment in a rela-tionship with another woman.

Which brings us to Mary Rozet Smith, who brought "Love" into Jane Addams's life as Starr, apparently, had not. Am I seriously arguing that these two women's forty-year love affair was not erotic? Would I suggest a non-physical scenario if the bond were heterosexual? No, I would not because law and custom dictated the rules of a heterosexual married life for Addams's generation. In the late nineteenth and early twentieth centuries, however, there were no such rules for two loving women; they could make it up as they wished. And the work of modern historians of sexuality makes clear that, left to their own devices, free of the patriarchal dictates governing reproduction and inheritance, individuals occupy an infinite array of places along a continuum of sexual expression, from highly physical to not physical at all, from heterosexual to bisexual to homosexual. As Carroll Smith-Rosenberg argued back in 1975, "sexual and emotional impulses [are] part of a continuum or spectrum of affect gradations strongly influenced by cultural norms and arrangements." Smith-Rosenberg's point was that American women in the mid-nineteenth century defined "sex" as that which one did with men, so whatever women did together was, by definition, not sex.[19] Subsequently, the research of historians like Lillian Faderman and Leila Rupp has demonstrated that female partners could be devoted, loving, sentimental, and romantic without engaging in physical sex. As Rupp has argued, we need to "make distinctions among different sorts of women's relationships in the past without denying their significance or assigning fixed categories."[20]

In the case of Jane Addams and Mary Rozet Smith, the evidence prevents me from confidently assigning a fixed category but compels me to underscore the significance of the relationship in Addams's life. Stipulating to a Hull-House resident's prescient observation in 1894 that "J.A. could not live without" Mary, I can imagine two different sexual scenarios for these loving life partners, both of which fit the overall story of Jane Addams's development, personality, and political ideology.[21]

In the first scenario, Jane emerges as a sexually expressive adult through her love of Mary. That scenario perfectly fits the plot of my book: that Jane Addams had to change and grow and struggle to become a person capable of genuine connection with others, genuine intimacy with others. Though emotionally elusive and self-protective as a young woman, she became, through the life and love she chose in Chicago, a much more warm, emotionally available, intimate person. It would make sense that sexual expression would go along with this personal evolution.

In the second scenario, Jane evolves into a more emotionally available person but continues to find psychological safety in holding herself slightly aloof from everyday life, always poised and self-possessed, above the embodied fray and just a bit disdainful of our "puny" and "perishable flesh." That scenario invites the question: was Jane attracted to Mary because she ignited the sexual flame that Ellen had failed to light. . . or was Jane drawn to Mary because Mary did not make the demands Ellen made for emotional and erotic expression, demands that Jane Addams could never bring herself satisfy?

Included in Jane Addams's papers are 465 letters between her and Mary, but that epistolary record does not yield up all that one would wish. In the last year of her life, while assembling her papers for the nephew who was writing her biography, Addams reported that she had destroyed over half of her correspondence with Mary on the grounds that it was "much too intimate" to be of use to a biographer.[22] Curiously and, I think significantly, she does not seem to have destroyed the early letters, the courtship letters, which contain sincere expressions of affection, even devotion, but contain no kisses or beds. We are left to wonder just what was too intimate in the letters Addams destroyed—expressions of physical longing or candid remarks on friends and family?

Our desire to know whether the sexual or non-sexual scenario most closely captures Jane Addams's lived experience need not arise from a hunger for sexual gossip. We engage in biographical study of people in the past in order to learn more about the complexities of the human condition. As part of that project, we collect data on sexual expression in order to understand just how fixed and just how variable it is. When we confront individuals in history like Jane Addams and Mary Rozet Smith, women who clearly loved each other with all their hearts but did not leave any traces of sexual expression, we quite appropriately want to know if their experience reflects women's capacity for erotic expression in a culture that did not encourage such expression or reflects women's capacity to experience great love without the erotic, especially in a culture that valorized women, even empowered women, for being sexually self-disciplined. These are wholly legitimate historical questions, and anyone who regards them as unseemly should get her own head out of the gutter.

Alongside our general historical interest in human beings' sexual and emotional malleability, there is a very particular reason for wanting to know about Jane Addams's sexual experience. Her daily life in the Hull-House neighborhood put her in contact with young working-class people whose sexual mores were rapidly diverging from those of their parents—or from those Addams regarded as safe and respectable. Living and working in the city in the early decades of the twentieth century, with money in their pockets and plenty of places to spend it, young men and women were going to dance halls and nickleodeons, frequenting beer gardens and amusement parks, walking the streets unchaperoned, necking and petting in alleyways.[23] It was vital to Addams's reform project to reach young people and engage them in union activity, civic activity, and charitable activity, and it does appear that she was successful at dealing with socially conservative, foreign-born young adults. But the question arises: was Jane Addams's lifelong inability to understand the joyful, irrational abandon of sexuality an impediment to her establishing a connection with the American-born adolescents and young adults in her neighborhood? When she was no longer dealing with sexually conservative immigrants but, instead, sexually adventurous ethnic workers, did she reach the limit of her ability to identify with the Other, to liberally embrace other ways of operating?

These are genuine questions. I raise them here to illustrate that curiosity about Addams's sexuality arises quite appropriately from curiosity about her ability to achieve her own reform goals. The personal in her case, as in everyone's case, had political dimensions, so it would be useful to know more about the personal.

In the absence of material on the personal, we turn to Addams's expressions of a sexual ideology in her published writings. In *Spirit of Youth and the City Streets,* which came out in 1909, Addams spoke of a "fundamental sex susceptibility which suffuses the world with its deepest meaning and beauty," but she made clear her belief that youthful sexual energy could and should be harnessed to more elevated pursuits: the arts, social reform, and philanthropy.[24] Three years later, in her uncharacteristically sensationalistic book on prostitution, *A New Conscience and an Ancient Evil,* Addams gave full voice to her belief that indulgence in sexuality outside of traditional marriage was a form of selfishness, that progress toward a harmonious, communal society required that individuals channel their selfishness into more spiritual forms of expression, and that women were more morally and sexually suited than men to lead society in that direction.[25]

Does the evidence from Jane Addams's writings prove that she did not engage in erotic activity with Mary Rozet Smith, that her seminary views of sexuality as a foolish and wasteful indulgence persisted into adulthood? Do her writings suggest that, like the mid–nineteenth-century women Carroll Smith-Rosenberg talked about, Addams simply defined sex as what women did with men and believed sex could only be elevated above selfishness and capitalist exploitation if regulated by women within marriage? Does it suggest that, like plenty of other women of her generation, Addams could advance an ideal of a feminized, spiritualized society while still enjoying erotic expression?

The questions hang heavy in the air, like the questions Jane Addams and I occasionally ask each other in my office or in my car. They are never answered, and I doubt they ever will be. But even without firm answers, the questions have much to teach us. The mere fact of these questions serves as a reminder that human sexuality is a fluid capacity, always morphing, utterly pliable. In the

71

context of my very long-distance relationship with Addams, a woman so famously self-possessed that her own nephew described her as "impersonal," the difficulty with defining her sexuality has only served to further impress upon me what a complicated, emotionally elusive, somewhat manipulative but always attractive personality she was.[26] Of course, plenty of individuals fitting that description have been sexual in garden-variety ways. But Addams is not garden-variety; she refuses to be squeezed into any standard categories of politics, religion, career, or domestic life. Why should she conform to sexual categorization?

I have given myself up to the mystery of Jane Addams, refusing to feign certitude about the presence or absence of the erotic in her intimate life because I do not want to presume that much familiarity or suggest to anyone that she is that easy to know. I think we learn more about her and ourselves if we admit the unpredictability of love and sex and intimacy and allow this part of Addams's life to serve as a signifier for that which is curious, mysterious, annoying, and compelling about the very queer head resident of Hull-House.

ENDNOTES

1. "The Only Saint America Has Produced," *Current Literature* 40 (April 1906): 377–79.

2. Victoria Bissell Brown, *The Education of Jane Addams* (Philadelphia: University of Pennsylvania Press, 2004), 62.

3. Ellen Gates Starr to Jane Addams, October 22, 1882. Swarthmore College Peace Collection.

4. Ellen Gates Starr to Jane Addams, March 14, 1888, and March 17 and 18, 1888. Sarah Alice Haldeman Papers, Lilly Library, Indiana University.

5. Jane Addams, *Twenty Years at Hull-House with Autobiographical Notes* (New York: The Macmillan Company, 1910), 94.

6. Jane Addams to Ellen Gates Starr, January 24, 1889. Ellen Gates Starr Papers, Smith College Archives. Jane Addams to Alice Haldeman Addams, August 31, 1889. Jane Addams Memorial Collection, University of Illinois Special Collections.

7. Jane Addams, "A Retrospect," Fall, 1895. Swarthmore College Peace Collection. Addams wrote this poem while convalescing from typhoid fever. To thank Mary Smith for taking care of Addams during the illness, she gave her a book by Charles Lamb and wrote in an accompanying, undated note that she wished "there was some book that would express all the gratitude and affection I have for you. I fear I will have to write one myself to get it all in." Jane Addams to Mary Rozet Smith, n.d., Swarthmore College Peace Collection.

8. For a fuller discussion of the two women's daily lives, see Brown, *The Education of Jane Addams*, 253–59.

9. Jane Addams, undated poem to Mary Rozet Smith, Swarthmore College Peace Collection.

10. James Weber Linn, *Jane Addams: A Biography* (New York: D. Appleton-Century, 1935), 149.

11. Mary Rozet Smith to Jane Addams, September 3, 1933. Swarthmore College Peace Collection.

12. Margaret Dreier Robins to Jane Addams, March 1, 1934. Swarthmore College Peace Collection. Jane referred to Mary's death as "the day of my downfall," and many friends anticipated that the already-ailing Jane would not survive the loss of Mary. Jane Addams to Lillian Wald, September 30, 1934. Lillian Wald Papers, New York Public Library. See, too, Grace Abbott to Jane Addams, February 22, 1934, regarding her "fear" of the "possible effects" of Mary's death on Jane. Swarthmore College Peace Collection. Mary Lewis Langworthy described Mary's death as an "almost unbearable loss" for Jane and Graham Taylor told Jane it was "the greatest loss you could suffer." Langworthy to Addams, February 23, 1934; Taylor to Addams, February 23, 1934. Swarthmore College Peace Collection.

13. Blanche Wiesen Cook defined lesbians as "women who love women, who choose women to nurture and support" in "Female Support Networks and Political Activism: Lillian Wald, Crystal Eastman, Emma Goldman," *Chrysalis* 3 (Autumn 1977): 43–61. This pioneering definition significantly contributed to the process by which historians came to understand the cultural construction of emotional and sexual life. At the same time, however, the term "lesbian" was being constructed as a reference to sexual, not merely emotional, preference. As historians have come to recognize that sexual expression is subject to historical and cultural change, we have become more cautious about assuming that we know what individuals' sexual conduct was in the past.

14. Nancy Sahli, "Smashing: Women's Relationships before the Fall," *Chrysalis* 8 (1979): 18–27; Vallie Beck to Jane Addams, October 4, 1877. Swarthmore College Peace Collection. Jane Addams, "Editorial," *Rockford Seminary Magazine* 9 (February 1881): 88.

15. Jane Addams to Ellen Gates Starr, August 11, 1879. Ellen Gates Starr Papers, Smith College Archives. This letter is an early indication of Jane's youthful need to deflect sentiment, for Ellen had dropped out of Rockford Female Seminary and Jane was bluntly explaining to her "beloved friend" that she was sorry to think their friendship was over but felt it best that people "honestly" go on with their separate lives; "don't need to 'descend' you know."

16. Jane Addams, "Darkness vs. Nebulae," June 14, 1880, Rockford Seminary essays, Detzer Collection, University of Illinois. For similar ideas, see "The Nebular Hypothesis," January 28, 1880, Rockford Seminary essays, Detzer Collection, University of Illinois.

73

17. Jane Addams, "What I Think, That I Am," undated Rockford Seminary essays, Detzer Collection, University of Illinois. Jane Addams to Ellen Gates Starr, January 29, 1880. Ellen Gates Starr Papers, Smith College Archives.

18. Jane Addams to Ellen Gates Starr, January 7, 1883. Ellen Gates Starr Papers, Smith College Archives. Jane Addams to Alice Addams Haldeman, March 18 and 22, 1888, Sarah Alice Haldeman Papers, Lilly Library, Indiana University.

19. Carroll Smith-Rosenberg, "The Female World of Love and Ritual," *Signs* 1 (Autumn 1975): 43–61.

20. Leila Rupp, "'Imagine My Surprise': Women's Relationships in Historical Perspective," *Frontiers: A Journal of Women's Studies* 5 (Fall 1980): 62. See, too, Leila Rupp, *A Desired Past: A Short History of Same-Sex Love in America* (Chicago: University of Chicago Press, 1999); Lillian Faderman, "Boston Marriages as a Possible Lesson for Today," *Boston Marriages: Romantic but Asexual Relationships among Contemporary Lesbians,* ed. Esther D. Rothblum and Kathleen A. Brehony (Amherst: University of Massachusetts Press, 1993), 29–42. As is obvious from the title of this book, not everyone who studies sexuality and its history agrees that the term "lesbian" should be reserved for sexual relations. The literature on the history of sexuality is now vast. A sample of relevant works includes Lillian Faderman, *Surpassing the Love of Men: Romantic Friendship and Love between Women from the Renaissance to the Present* (New York: Morrow, 1981); Noel Riley Fitch, "The Elusive 'Seamless Whole': A Biographer Treats (or Fails to Treat) Lesbianism," *Lesbian Texts and Contexts: Radical Revisions,* eds. Karla Jay and Joanne Glasgow (New York: New York University Press, 1990); Nancy S. Landale and Avery M. Guest, "Ideology and Sexuality among Victorian Women," *Social Science History* 19 (Summer 1986): 147–70; Karen Lystra, *Searching the Heart: Women, Men, and Romantic Love in Nineteenth-Century America* (New York: Oxford University Press, 1989); Steven Seidman, "The Power of Desire and the Danger of Pleasure: Victorian Sexuality Reconsidered," *Journal of Social History* 24 (Fall 1990): 47–67; Estelle Freedman, "Sexuality in Nineteenth-Century America: Behavior, Ideology, and Politics," *Reviews in American History* (December 1982): 196–215.

21. Alice Hamilton to Edith Hamilton, February 23, 1894, in *Alice Hamilton: A Life in Letters* (Cambridge: Harvard University Press, 1984), 347.

22. Jane Addams to James Weber Linn, March 8, 1935. Swarthmore College Peace Collection.

23. The literature on youth, sexuality, and urban life in the early twentieth century is quite rich. See, for example, Kathy Peiss, *Cheap Amusements: Working Women and Leisure in Turn-of-the-Century New York* (Philadelphia: Temple University Press, 1986); Joanne Meyerowitz, *Women Adrift: Independent Wage Earners in Chicago, 1880-1930* (Chicago: University of Chicago Press, 1988); Elizabeth Alice Clement, *Love for Sale: Courting, Treating, and Prostitution in New York City, 1900-1945* (Chapel Hill: University of North Carolina Press, 2006); Nan Enstad, *Ladies of Labor, Girls of Adventure: Working Women, Popular Culture, and Labor Politics at the Turn of the Twentieth Century* (New York: Columbia University Press, 1999); Sharon Wood, *The*

74

Freedom of the Streets: Work, Citizenship, and Sexuality in a Gilded Age City (Chapel Hill: University of North Carolina Press, 2005); Lauren Rabinovitz, *For the Love of Pleasure: Women, Movies, and Culture in Turn-of-the-Century Chicago* (New Brunswick, N.J.: Rutgers University Press, 1998); Sharon R. Ullman, *Sex Seen: The Emergence of Modern Sexuality in America* (Berkeley: University of California Press, 1997); Sarah E. Chinn, *Inventing Modern Adolescence: The Children of Immigrants in Turn-of-the-Century America* (New Brunswick, N.J.: Rutgers University Press, 2008).

24. Jane Addams, *Spirit of Youth and the City Streets* (New York: The Macmillan Company, 1909), 16.

25. For an extended discussion of *A New Conscience and an Ancient Evil,* see Victoria Bissell Brown, "Sex and the City: Jane Addams Confronts Prostitution," *Feminist Interpretations of Jane Addams,* ed. Maurice Hamington.(University Park: The Pennsylvania State University Press, 2010): 126–57.

26. James Weber Linn to Ellen Gates Starr, May 4, 1935. Ellen Gates Starr Papers, Smith College Archives.

ON THE GAY SIDE OF TOWN
Chicago's Homosexual Subculture
before World War II

Gregory Sprague

Editors' note: Greg Sprague's intellectual passion lay in digging up gay history and sharing it with as many people as possible. Born in 1951, in rural Kewanee, Illinois, Sprague attended Augustana College, received his first Master's in History from Purdue, and his second in Education from Indiana University. Degrees in hand, in 1977 Sprague moved to Chicago, entered a Ph.D. program in Education at Loyola University, and began to research and write a history of gay life in Chicago at the turn of the twentieth century. Unlike the urban historians around him who likely never thought much about sexuality or writing for an audience of non-academics, Sprague consciously converted his historical research into a travelling slide show that pictured the development of modern homosexuality, the gay rights movement, and Chicago's sexual underground. Taking the production of gay history one step further, Sprague founded the Chicago Gay and Lesbian History Project to create a clearinghouse for the city's gay past, and continue the process of making history accessible to the public. In 1981, the project evolved and partially morphed into the Gerber/Hart Library and Archives, a community-based institution that remains one of the largest LGBT archives in the Midwest.

In the midst of all of his community-based projects, Sprague also poured energy into researching and writing gay and lesbian history for an academic audience. "On the Gay Side of Town" was produced out of this effort. Sprague undertook the writing of this piece at a moment when the academic world was cool, if not hostile, to the study of homosexuality. Writing before a single historical monograph on U.S. LGBT history had appeared in print, Sprague relied on the work of sociologists and anthropologists, and a few historians including Jeffrey Weeks, Randolph Trumbach, and Vern Bullough, to contextualize his work on Chicago's gay past.[1]

Sprague hit archival gold around 1980 when he found the manuscript collection of Ernest Burgess, a sociologist on the faculty at the University of Chicago from 1916 to 1952. Beginning in the 1930s, Burgess, who was well on this way to becoming the father of the Chicago School of Sociology, a field defined by the study of urban life's social and physical fabric, sent his students out into the city to perform ethnographic research on people who lived on the sexual and racial margins of Chicago. In the process, Burgess oversaw the training of dozens of graduate students as they collected some of the most detailed and explicit material on Chicagoans' sexual and social experiences in the pre-WWII era.[2] *For reasons we do not fully know, Burgess never published any of these findings on homosexuality, but he kept all of the research reports, which the University of Chicago acquired after his death in 1966. Almost twenty years later, Sprague found these reports and sifted through over 100 boxes of records, photocopying the ethnographically rich materials detailing the "gay" life of Chicago. Sprague used his findings to write a seminar paper for graduate school, and then tried to get it published in the* Journal of Urban History *and the* Journal of Social History, *two of the major academic journals in the field of history. As is the case with academic peer-reviewed work, several anonymous reviewers vetted Sprague's essay. In this case each suggested that the essay required revision before it could be accepted for publication. Despite their concerns, the reviewers acknowledged that Sprague was "sitting on a gold-mine" of research, which would potentially change the state of the nascent field of history of sexuality. Instead of substantially revising the piece, Sprague chose instead to limit his revisions and publish an abbreviated piece, which he then titled "Chicago Past: A Rich Gay History," in the* Advocate *in 1983. Even in this shortened form, the essay was among the first archival-based works on gay history ever published.*

78

Two years after "Chicago Past" appeared in print, Sprague was diagnosed with AIDS. He died two years later in 1987. Sprague's lover in the late 1970s, Walter Williams, now a professor at University of Southern California, remembers that before his death Sprague made a conscious decision to compile all of his research and writing and leave it to the Chicago History Museum. Since he knew he would never be able to write up everything he found before he died, he wanted to ensure that future researchers would. And use it they did. Sprague's collection of archival material and oral histories of gay and lesbians in Chicago is one of CHM's most requested collections. In 1997, a decade after Sprague's death, the first wave of publications appeared that used the Burgess collection and other sources that Sprague found. In Interzones, *one of the first published texts that dealt with the history of queer Chicago, author Kevin Mumford cited Sprague's unpublished scholarly essay and relied heavily on the Burgess collection, which he likely read about in Sprague's work. In the years since and even now, historians have repeatedly relied on the papers of Ernest Burgess, the Committee of Fifteen, and the Juvenile Protective Association to understand queer life in Chicago, all of which Sprague vetted.[3]*

In the pages that follow you will read a version of Sprague's essay, "On the Gay Side of Town." We have posthumously published this essay to honor a historian who fundamentally shaped our project of writing and exhibiting Chicago's queer past.

The editors wish to acknowledge the assistance of Anne Parsons and Jessica Herczeg-Konecny in the preparation of this essay.

ENDNOTES

1. Jeffrey Weeks, "Inverts, Perverts, and Mary-Annes: Male Prostitution and the Regulation of Homosexuality in England in the Nineteenth and Early Twentieth Centuries," *Journal of Homosexuality*, 6 (December 1981), 113-134 ; Randolph Trumbach, "London's Sodomites: Homosexual Behavior and Western Culture in the 18th Century," Journal of Social History vol. 11, no. 1 (1977): 1-33; and Vern Bullough, *Sexual Variance in Society and History* (New York: John Wiley and Sons, 1976). Sprague also used the documentary history, Jonathan Katz, ed., *Gay American History: Lesbian and Gay Men in the United States* (New York: Crowell, 1976).

2. For a more extensive discussion of sexuality and race in the Chicago School see Chad Heap, "The City as Sexual Laboratory: The Queer Heritage of the Chicago School," *Qualitative Sociology, Vol. 26, No. 4, Winter 2003*, 457-487, and Roderick Ferguson, *Aberrations in Black: Towards a Queer Critique of Color* (University of Minnesota, 2004).

3. Kevin J. Mumford, Interzones: *Black/White Sex Districts in Chicago and New York in the Early Twentieth Century* (New York: Columbia University Press, 1997); David Johnson, "Kids of Fairytown: Gay Male Culture on Chicago's Near North Side," in Brett Beemyn, *Creating a Place for Ourselves: Lesbian, Gay and Bisexual Community Histories* (New York, Routledge: 1997), 97-118; Allen Drexel, "Before Paris Burned: Race, Class, and Male Homosexuality on the Chicago South Side, 1935-1960" in *Creating a Place for Ourselves*, 119-144; and Chad Heap, *Slumming: Sexual and Racial Encounters in American Nightlife, 1885-1940* (Chicago: The University of Chicago Press, 2009).

Throughout its history, Chicago has been depicted as a place of great temptation. During the nineteenth century, the city acquired a special reputation for being very wild, corrupt, and vice-ridden. The image of Chicago as a city where young men were easily seduced from the path of righteousness into a life of sin and sexual debauchery was common among country folk and moral reformers at the turn of the century. These reformers quickly pointed out how the anonymity of the city allowed for the growth of "illicit sexual outlets."

The Chicago Vice Commission, established to investigate the urban sexual underground, reported in 1911 on the difficulty of controlling sexual behavior "in a city the size of Chicago." (In 1880, Chicago had a population of over one million; and by 1930, the population had tripled to three million.) The members of the Commission concluded that an individual living in Chicago could essentially "live any life he please, so far as his personal habits are concerned, and no one be the wiser." As it turned out, many of these men chose a gay lifestyle.

Chicago's rapid urbanization allowed a complex and varied gay male subculture to take root and grow from the 1880s to the 1930s. Urbanization created the necessary anonymous environment that allowed men who participated in socially stigmatized homosexual behavior to secretively meet, interact, and construct a subculture of their own. This submerged gay social world developed its own social institutions, patterns of behavior, sense of identity, specialized linguistic code, and even a folk literature.

Chicago has a long tradition of homosexual activity. Early European explorers condemned the common practice of sodomy among the Illinois and Miami Indians who lived on the western shores of Lake Michigan where Chicago would later stand. In the 1850s, only two decades after the incorporation of Chicago as a city, "male degenerates" were reported to have been quite active in the wild sexual underground of this frontier city. By 1889, a Chicago physician named G. Frank Lydston acknowledged the existence of homosexual subcultures in large American cities like Chicago: "There is in every community of any size a colony of male sexual perverts; they are usually known to each other, and are likely to congregate together. . . . they operate in accordance with some definite and concerted plan in quest of subjects wherewith to gratify their abnormal sexual impulses."

Another Chicago doctor, James G. Kiernan, a major American collaborator on Havelock Ellis's pioneer study of homosexuality *Sexual Inversion* (England, 1897), filled in some of the details of this urban "world of sexual inverts." Kiernan described this community as "distinctly organized—words, customs, traditions of its own" with a variety of public meeting places including "certain churches where inverts congregate; certain cafes well known for the inverted character of their patrons; certain streets where, at night every fifth man is an invert." According to Kiernan, common social institutions of the subculture in the 1890s included the "invert clubs" that were "really dancehalls attached to saloons, and presided over by an invert" and his "inverted" staff of waiters and musicians.

Still another physician from Chicago, William Held, writing in 1905, confirmed Kiernan's earlier findings. Held, in his published tract on the nature of homosexuality, mentioned several meeting places of Chicago gay men including "a church on X avenue, which seems to be a promenade for perverts at certain hours" and "a basement saloon on X street" where reportedly on Saturdays "at least fifty perverts were present." Held also testified that male prostitutes in Chicago were "almost as easy access as the female puellae." On certain streets at specific times, these boys and young men would often approach other males "under the pretense of begging for a night's lodging."

Male prostitution played a significant role in the early stages of the developing gay subculture, because the male prostitute often lived most of his life in the subculture while other men with homosexual desires spent only a small part of their daily lives interacting with homosexual individuals in gay environments. Jeffrey Weeks found a similar pattern in the gay subculture of nineteenth-century London where professional male prostitutes were "perhaps the only people who lived wholly in the subculture" and incorporated "sexual mores, social activities, and public identity into a full-time homosexual 'way of life'."[1] This centrality of male prostitution to gay subcultures lessened over time as the subculture matured and became more complex and varied in its composition. By the 1920s and 1930s, men in Chicago other than prostitutes were developing gay identities and spending large amounts of their leisure time in the subculture by participating in public gay institutions such as bars and baths, or by primarily interacting with other gay men through friendship networks.

During the first decade of the 20th century, the practice and art of prostitution reached its zenith in Chicago. Both female and male prostitution appear to have been a common occupation in the Windy City. Much of the prostitution at this time could be found in the wonderfully decadent Levee, a vice district just south of the downtown Loop. The vice-ridden Levee was under the special protection of the corrupt pair of political bosses—Michael "Hinky Dink" Kenna and "Bathhouse" John Coughlin—who received large contributions from local madams and pimps. An abundance of brothels and gambling dens flourished not only in the Levee but throughout the city.

By 1910 the good citizens of Chicago, even with their tolerance for vice, corrupt politicians, and crime lords, could no longer ignore the widespread prostitution and the other sexual irregularities in their fair city. A group of influential clergymen pressured the crooked Mayor Fred A. Busse to appoint a commission to study vice in Chicago "with a view of determining a plan of control as well as considering the moral and physical harm which results from vice." The Chicago Vice Commission was one of many such civic commissions established in the early twentieth century to investigate what moral reformers considered the phenomenal growth of prostitution and other related "evils" in the large urban centers of the United States.

Early in its investigation, the attention of the Commission "was called by several persons to the practice of sexual perversion which was said to be very prevalent and growing in Chicago." Judicial and law enforcement authorities also confirmed this impression of growing homosexual activity in the city. A psychiatrist on the Commission was assigned the task of following up on these reports of "perversion." He sent out one of his medical students, who appeared to have had some contact with the gay subculture, to investigate the "homosexual underground." When the student reported back to the Commission, his stories of widespread homosexuality as well as his "lurid facts" caused the Commission to doubt the accuracy of his investigation.

The Commission then acquired a special investigator from New York City to do a followup investigation on homosexuality in Chicago. The medical student recommended that the new man from New York put on "a red tie and walk down the east side of State Street between four and five in the afternoon and see what happens." The astonished investigator, with "his hair almost standing on end," returned to the Commission after his walk down State Street and reported that he was approached by fifteen to twenty men who wanted to have sex with him. Around the turn of the century, gay men often wore red neckties as a means of identification on the city streets, making contacts for same-sex encounters easier and less dangerous.

In the end, the Commission collected a large amount of data on the gay subculture in Chicago, including an estimate of twenty thousand active homosexuals living in the city. It discovered several rooming houses whose residents were mostly young gay men often "of the counter jumper variety (dry goods, sales people)" who reportedly would sometimes put on women's clothes for the night. Large department stores like Marshall Field's appeared to have had a large workforce of gay clerks or "counterjumpers" at the turn of the century. (This tradition in Chicago department stores continues up to today.) Public gay meeting places were also reported, including "notorious saloons" with female impersonators and a large music hall with "a much applauded act . . . of a man who by facial expression and bodily contortion represented sex perversion, a most disgusting performance." A specialized gay language with a corresponding folk literature and music were noted in the report:

> They have a vocabulary and signs of recognition of their own, which serve as an introduction into their own society. The cult has produced some literature, much of which is uncomprehensible [sic] to one who cannot read between the lines . . . one of the songs recently ruled off the stage by the police department was inoffensive to innocent ears, but was really written by a member of the cult, and replete with suggestiveness to those who understand the language of the group.

The Vice Commission also acknowledged that homosexuality existed among all social classes in Chicago. Its report primarily focused on middle-class gay men, because its investigator was "unable to gain entrance into those circles of the very well-to-do, which are engaged in these practices, nor did he concern himself with the lowest stratum of society, which is the class most observable on our courts." Homosexuality was just as prevalent, however, among the wealthy and the destitute as among the middle class.

Upper-class gay men often developed their separate friendship networks and their own subcultural institutions, which provided special protection and privacy not always available to the other classes of gay men. Private clubs and all-male residential hotels served as gay institutions for the more discreet and well-to-do gay man. These clubs often passed as athletic societies, chess clubs, or dramatic societies.

The Chicago Athletic Club during the 1910s and 1920s functioned in part as a residential club for wealthy gay men. An informant who worked at the

Athletic Club during this period reported that a large group of club members (including a doctor, university professor, and a major stockholder in the Chicago Stock Yards) had rooms at the Club and had regular homosexual relations with adolescent boys and young men within the protective environment of the Athletic Club. Certain exclusive restaurants also served as discreet meeting places for Chicago's gay elite. Gerard's, a restaurant on State Street just south of the Loop, was reported by a patron to be a popular gathering place for wealthy gay men around 1920, including members of the recently exiled German royal family.

Significant homosexual activity was present in even Chicago's lowest social strata: the "hobos." During the early decades of the twentieth century, Chicago, the hub of the nation's rail system, became a major center for homeless men. A 1923 study of this culture by a University of Chicago sociologist stated "that homosexual practices among homeless men are widespread" and "are especially prevalent among homeless men on the road among whom there is a tendency to idealize and justify the practice."[2] In Chicago, a regular pattern of homosexual encounters and relationships developed in the many flop-houses of the slum districts and in the city parks. Grant Park on the lakefront was known for its "fresh air camps" of homeless where "homosexual associations and practices" existed among homeless men and runaway youths.

After the Vice Report of 1911, authorities tried to clean up vice in Chicago. The reformers broke up major vice districts like the Levee, but this essentially just dispersed prostitution and other related activities throughout the city. No evidence suggests any systematic effort to "round-up" homosexuals or suppress their subcultural institutions. By the 1920s, the powers-that-be in Chicago had little desire to control vice and "illicit sexual activity." During much of this decade, the city government was under the control of the colorful Republican Mayor "Big Bill" Thompson and his corrupt political machine, which had close ties to the Chicago criminal underground and their vice interests.

Although Prohibition was in effect, gay dancehalls and speakeasies flourished alongside establishments that catered to heterosexuals. One popular gay dancehall during this era was Diamond Lil's, named after a Mae West play running in New York around 1928. Diamond Lil's patrons were described as being "extremely Bohemian" but with a good number of college men who all danced together in the backroom. The outlandish manager of the dancehall adopted the name Diamond Lil as his own and always wore a red tie with a huge imitation diamond stickpin.

During the '20s and '30s, Thompson's, a chain of Chicago restaurants, also attracted a large gay clientele. Two of these restaurants (one in the Loop and the other on the Near North Side) became known as places where gay men would socialize and cruise for sexual partners. Although the Dill Pickle Club, also on the Near North Side, was not a strictly gay establishment, many of the younger gay intellectual and artistic crowd would "hang out" at that bohemian dive. This same "artistic" crowd haunted the Art Institute, the Chicago Opera, Orchestra Hall, and the various art, music and dance studios around the Loop and the Near North.

By the 1920s, a significant number of gay men lived and frequented the Near North neighborhood around the old Chicago Water Tower. The neighborhood also featured many gay hangouts. The area became known as Towertown: an artistic and "morally loose" bohemian village similar to New York's Greenwich Village. Towertown hosted many gay friendship networks as well as large private parties of gay men and lesbians. An even more submerged black gay community with its own institutions grew up on the South Side about the same period, with close ties to the growing jazz culture in Chicago.

As Chicago in the 1920s saw a major expansion of the gay subculture, it also saw the origins of the gay rights movement in the United States. On December 10, 1924, postal worker Henry Gerber received from the State of Illinois a Charter of Incorporation for his Society for Human Rights: the first American gay rights organization. Gerber and a handful of gay men from Chicago founded the Society for Human Rights to "ameliorate the plight of homosexuals in America." Gerber had been profoundly influenced by the German homosexual emancipation movement he had witnessed during his military duty in post–World War I Germany.

Although Gerber received little support from the Chicago gay subculture, he had high hopes for his small organization. Gerber wanted to attract to the Society a large number of gay people who would be urged to refrain from behavior considered offensive to the general public. He hoped "through self-discipline, homophiles would win the confidence and assistance of legal authorities and legislators in understanding the problem; that these authorities should be educated on the futility and folly of long prison terms for committing homosexual acts, etc." Through the Society's publication *Friendship and Freedom*, Gerber hoped to reach a large portion of the submerged gay community who might support the group's goals.

But Gerber only published two editions of *Friendship and Freedom* before the Chicago police harassed the Society out of existence. In the summer of 1925, Chicago police arrested Henry Gerber and the other officers of the Society and essentially destroyed this early gay rights organization. After three trials and the loss of his Post Office job, Gerber's case was finally dismissed in the courts. No one from the Chicago gay subculture came to his defense, and Gerber saw himself as a martyr "for the cause of homosexuality." Like most urban gay subcultures in the United States at this time, it was not mature or threatened enough to take on the burden of a homosexual rights campaign. That would have to wait until after 1950.

With the onset of the Great Depression in 1929, city living, in general, became much more difficult. But in the early 1930s, the Chicago gay subculture appeared to have been thriving in the midst of great economic distress. A multitude of gay institutions and friendship networks flourished during these years with little interference from the local authorities who could not have been ignorant of large scale and fairly open activities by such a stigmatized and supposedly "criminal" group. At times, the Chicago gay subculture appeared to have received special protection from the police, especially during the large public gay masquerades or "drags."

In the 1930s, gay men had many public meeting places, including restaurants, bars, Turkish baths, parks, and restrooms. The more anonymous places included four bathhouses on the North Side, especially Jacks at Dearborn and Walton, that would allow same-sex encounters within their premises. Public parks like Bughouse Square (Washington Park), Lincoln Park, and the Oak Street Beach served as contact points for men desiring sex with other men. A host of public toilets became "notorious" for homosexual activity, including men's restrooms at several railway stations and one in the Chicago Public Library.

The city also featured public institutions for gay socializing. Along with Thompson's Restaurants, Henrici's was a restaurant known for its high-class gay clientele. Other known gay nightclubs included the Casino Club, La Masque, Sally's Shoppe, and the popular Bally Hoo Cafe. The Bally Hoo on North Halsted Street had a reputation for being a very hot nightspot, with entertainment including a popular lesbian hostess (who dressed in masculine style) and a gay MC (often appearing in drag) named "Mack and Marge."

Another popular gay couple, Frankie and Johnnie (both males) performed at the Bally Hoo as well as at other gay nightclubs and private parties. Gay audiences loved their campy jokes and songs in the slang of the period:

Father Spanish, Mother Greek and I'm French

They call me Del Monte because I'm the sweetest Fruit in town.

Fairytown, Fairytown, that's where all the boys go down.

Whoops! My dear,
Whoops! My dear, even the Chief of Police is queer.

When the sailors come to town –
Lots of brown, lots of brown.

Holy by Jesus
Everybody got pareses in Fairy Town.

By the 1930s, the Chicago subculture had developed a complex and rich specialized vocabulary. Some subcultural terms emphasized the difference between homosexuals and heterosexuals. Homosexuals used terms like "gay," "queer," and "tempermental" to differentiate themselves from heterosexuals, who were often called "jam." Many words highlighted particular types of people, locales, mannerisms, and acts found in the gay subculture. Labels like "queen," "belle," "pansy," and "marge" described effeminate men. An older gay man who was interested in younger men was called "Auntie." "Bulldagger" and "mente" meant lesbian. "Dirt" was a sex partner who would later blackmail or harm a gay individual. Of course, a "tearoom" was a public restroom where sexual contact was made. Words like "butch" (masculine characteristics) and "swishy" (effeminate gestures) labeled subcultural mannerisms. "Plain sewing" (masturbation), "browning" (anal intercourse), and "Frenching" (fellatio) were all slang words for sex acts. A gay man of the period defined "coming out" as when "you realize that there are other tempermentals like yourself."

Members of Chicago's gay subculture also regularly attended public masquerade balls held at the Coliseum Annex (a public hall south of the Loop) twice a year with the approval of the city government. Chicago's masquerade balls were similar to homosexual "drags" held in Paris, Berlin, St. Louis, and New York's Harlem during the early decades of the twentieth century. A straight observer, attending a New Year's Eve ball in Chicago, commented on this remarkable event:

Twice a year, with the knowledge and protection of Chicago's officialdom, do the homosexuals of the city gather in great numbers for their semi-annual costume ball, at which conventions and repressions are flung to the winds. New Year's Eve and the Hallowe'en mark the occasions for the celebrations of the 'shadow world'.

The same observer remarked about this "unusual and colorful sight" of some five hundred gay people dancing and swaying to the music of a "colored" jazz orchestra as well an "unconventional sight" of "two handsome young men in street clothes dancing, cheek to cheek, holding one another in close embrace, as any girl and boy would at any dance." Nearly a thousand gay men and lesbians attended another masquerade ball on October 30, 1932, which lasted until 3:00 a.m. and featured many extremely exotic costumes.

These masquerade balls of the 1930s probably helped many gay individuals to identify more closely with others of the subculture. The gay balls, occasions for celebration in a usually hostile world, also reinforced the participants' gay identities and the cohesive security of the usually hidden subculture.

Of course, all men who participated in homosexual behavior in Chicago did not develop a gay identity. Individuals varied greatly in their involvement and commitment to the subculture. But a gay identity and group consciousness existed among many of the men who participated in the Chicago subculture. This group consciousness surpassed the self-awareness that their desire of same-sex relations made them different from the general population; it became an awareness that they belonged to a separate group of people that they themselves labeled gay. This special awareness can be seen in this brief excerpt from a love letter written in 1933 by a gay man in Baltimore to his friend Jimmy in Chicago: "Gay People are generally people who live their own lives, speak their own thoughts and are in love with their own sex."

By the time World War II exploded in 1941, Chicago's gay subculture had become a fairly stable cultural unit with its own institutions, social patterns, language, and even a folk literature. But the existence of this complex and "deviant" cultural entity was not widely known outside those worldly wise urbanites who occasionally came in contact with the subculture. The mass media (newspapers, radio and the movies) had censored most references to gays and their world. This ignorance gave the subculture a certain protection.

This situation began to change in the late '30s when police raids on gay bars increased. As Samuel Steward suggested, "the umbrella (of secrecy) began to become more and more dilapidated" by World War II. With the influx of military personnel into the city and into gay night spots, the pressure by the authorities on the gay institutions increased. Raids on gay bars and entrapments in the parks became commonplace. After the war with the rise of McCarthyism and the widespread knowledge (via Kinsey) that homosexuals were everywhere, the once fairly hidden and tolerated gay subculture in Chicago came under attack from all quarters. By the 1950s, many of the older gay men were longing for those "good old days" before World War II.

Notes on Sources: Much of the historical information found in this article was gathered through oral interviews with older gay men as well as from archive collections of personal letters and contemporary accounts of gay life in Chicago before 1940.

Acknowledgments: I wish to thank the following friends and colleagues who have either assisted with my research or by their example have inspired my work: Allan Berube, Eric Garber, Anne Juhasz, Jonathan Katz, Marie Kuda, Jim Monahan and Allan Spear. I also want to acknowledge the special support and encouragement that I have received from members of the Chicago Gay and Lesbian History Project, and the Lesbian and Gay Academic Union of Chicago.

89

A note on language: The word gay, in this study, is used as a descriptive term for men who were conscious that their erotic preference for their own sex made them different from the general population of heterosexual males (identity formation), and for their distinctive social institutions and cultural elements. The word homosexual, which is fairly restrictive and limited in usage (usually meaning sexual activities between the members of the same gender), is inadequate to describe the social structures and culture of gay males in urban America. And since the word gay does have a long heritage of usage by homosexual men, it is only logical for scholars writing on this type to adopt the terminology used by people they are investigating.

ENDNOTES
1. Jeffrey Weeks, "Inverts, Perverts, and Mary-Annes: Male Prostitution and the Regulation of Homosexuality in England in the Nineteenth and Early Twentieth Centuries," *Journal of Homosexuality* (Fall/Winter, 1980/81): 121.
2. Nels Anderson, *The Hobo – The Sociology of the Homeless Man* (Chicago: University of Chicago Press, 1923), 144.

APPENDIX

What follows is a bibliography of sources Gregory Sprague used to write his seminar paper, "On the 'Gay Side' of Town: The Nature and Structure of Male Homosexuality in Chicago, 1890-1935," at Loyola University of Chicago in 1982.

Anderson, Nels. *The Hobo—The Sociology of the Homeless Man*. Chicago: University of Chicago Press, 1923.

Binford, Jessie F. "The Year's Work—1925." In *Annual Report of the Juvenile Protective Association of Chicago*. Chicago: Juvenile Protective Association, 1926.

Boyer, Paul. *Urban Masses and Moral Order in America, 1820–1920*. Cambridge, MA: Harvard University Press, 1976.

Boyfrank, Manuel Collection, ONE National Gay & Lesbian Archives, Los Angeles, California.

Bruns, Roger A. *Knights of the Road: A Hobo History*. New York: Methuen, 1980.

Bullough, Vern L. *Sexual Variance in Society and History*. New York: John Wiley and Sons, 1976.

Bullough, Vern L. and Martha Voght. "Homosexuality and Its Confusion with the 'Secret Sin' in Pre-Freudian America." In *Sex, Society and History*, ed. Vern L. Bullough, 112–24. New York: Science History Publication, 1976.

Burgess, Ernest W. Papers, University of Chicago Library, Chicago, Illinois.

Burnham, John. "Early References to Homosexual Communities in American Medical Writings." *Medical Aspects of Human Sexuality* 8 (1973): 34–49.

Ellis, Havelock. *Studies in the Psychology of Sex: Volume II—Sexual Inversion*. New York: Random House, 1936 (reprint ed. of 1910).

Fisher, Claude S. "Theories of Urbanism." In *Urban Life: Readings in Urban Anthropology*, eds. George Gmelch and Walter Zenner. New York: St. Martin's Press, 1980.

Garber, Eric. "Tain't Nobody's Business: Homosexuality in Harlem in the 1920s," *The Advocate* 342 (1982): 41-42.

Gerber, Henry. "The Society for Human Rights—1925." *ONE Magazine* 9 (1962).

Grosskurth, Phyllis. *Havelock Ellis, A Biography*. New York: Alfred A. Knopf, 1980.

Haller, Mark. "Urban Vice and Civic Reform: Chicago in the Early Twentieth Century." In *Cities in American History*, eds. Kenneth T. Jackson and Stanley K. Schultz. New York: Alfred Knopf, 1972.

91

Healy, William Interview by John C. Burnham, January 1960, Chicago History Museum Research Center, Chicago, Illinois.

Held, William. *Crime, Habit or Disease? A Question of Sex from the Standpoint of Psychopathology.* Chicago, 1905.

Hirschfeld, Magnus. "Homosexuality in Philadelphia, Boston, Chicago, Denver, and New York." In *Gay American History: Lesbian and Gay Men in the United States*, ed. Jonathan Katz. New York: Crowell, 1976.

Hughes, Charles H. "Homo Sexual Complexion Perverts in St. Louis." In *Gay American History: Lesbian and Gay Men in the United States*, ed. Jonathan Katz. New York: Crowell, 1976.

Humphreys, Laud. "Exodus and Identity: The Emerging Gay Culture." In *Gay Men: The Sociology of Male Homosexuality*, ed. Martin P. Levine. New York: Harper and Row, 1979.

Humphreys, Laud and Brian Miller. "Identities in the Emerging Gay Culture." In *Homosexual Behavior: A Modern Reappraisal*, ed. Judd Marmor. New York: Basic Books, 1980.

Kiernan, James G. "Sexology…Classification of Homosexuality." *Urologic and Cutaneous Review* 6 (1916).

Lydston, G. Frank. Lecture on Sexual Perversion, Satyriasis, and Nymphomania. Reprinted in the *Philadelphia Medical and Surgical Report*. Chicago, 1889.

Mayne, Xavier (Edward Irenaus Prime Stevenson). *The Intersexes: A History of Similisexualism—as a Problem in Social Life.* Italy, 1980; reprint ed. New York: Arno Press, 1975.

Moon, Galen M. Interview by Gregory A. Sprague for the Chicago Gay and Lesbian History Project, August 25, 1980, Chicago History Museum Research Center, Chicago, Illinois.

Plummer, Kenneth. *Sexual Stigma: An Interactionist Account.* London: Routledge and Kegan Paul, 1975.

Rodgers, Bruce. *Gay Talk: A (Sometimes Outrageous) Dictionary of Gay Slang.* New York: Paragon Books, 1979.

Seilgman, Edwin R.A., ed. *The Social Evil with Special Reference to Conditions Existing in the City of New York: A Report Prepared (in 1902) under the Direction of the Committee of Fifteen*, 2nd ed. New York: G.P. Putnam's Sons, 1912.

Simon, William and John H. Gagnon. "Homosexuality: The Formation of a Sociological Perspective." In *The Same Sex: An Appraisal of Homosexuality*, ed. Ralph W. Weltse. Philadelphia: Pilgrim Press, 1969.

Smith, Robert Jerome. "Social Fold Custom: Festivals and Celebration." In *Folklore and Folklife*, ed. Richard M. Dorson. Chicago: University of Chicago Press, 1972.

Trumbach, Randolph. "London's Sodomites: Homosexual Behavior and Western Culture in the 18th Century." *Journal of Social History* 1 (1977): 1–33.

Vice Commission of Chicago. *The Social Evil in Chicago: A Study of Existing Conditions.* Chicago: Gunthorp-Warren, 1911.

Weeks, Jeffrey. "Inverts, Perverts, and Mary-Annes: Male Prostitution and the Regulation of Homosexuality in England in the Nineteenth and Early Twentieth Centuries." *Journal of Homosexuality* 1 & 2 (1980/81).

Weinberger, Constance and S.D. Alinsky. "The Public Dance Hall" (Unpublished paper) University of Chicago Library, Chicago, Illinois.

Zorbaugh, Harvey Warren. *The Gold Coast and the Slum: A Sociological Study of Chicago's Near North Side.* Chicago: The University of Chicago Press, 1929.

RETHINKING QUEER HISTORY
Or, Richard Nixon,
Gay Liberationist?[1]

John D'Emilio

My exploration of Chicago's queer history began as a small element of another project. I teach an undergraduate course called "Sexuality and Community," something like a "Gay 101." It introduces students to contemporary issues around sexual and gender identity. Since I am a historian by training and inclination, I spend the first chunk of the semester on history—a "where have we come from?" and "how did we get here?" prologue to the current issues we then explore.

Surprisingly, there is no short readable text to ground students quickly in this history. So, during a sabbatical semester a while back, I began pulling material together to write such a book. As new research, I decided to dip into Chicago sources. In United States historical writing, Chicago often functions as the representative example. Historians examining topics as diverse as labor radicalism, immigration, the New Deal, black migrations out of the South, urban political machines, and prostitution ground their research in Chicago and generalize from it. I imagined examples from Chicago as connecting tissue designed to make the text reader-friendly.

To my surprise, the more I dipped into Chicago's queer history, the more problematic I found it. I started to find things that did not confirm the common wisdom about gay and lesbian history. What I found and why this research surprised me is the subject of this essay. How do historians create our interpretations of the past? Where do those interpretations come from? How do historians figure out how to go beyond simple descriptions of what happened and instead give meaning to events?

To answer these questions, I will first offer a bit of the context that gave birth several decades ago to gay and lesbian–or queer–historical writing. Using examples, I will then summarize what the first generation of historians found. From there I will move on to my Chicago work, describing the ways in which I could easily bend and shape my findings to fit the older interpretive mold. Finally, through a particularly important and attention-grabbing example ("Richard Nixon, Gay Liberationist?"), I will explain how my research does not fit within those older frameworks and, instead, reveals a need for more expansive interpretive structures.

Gay and lesbian history was one of the byproducts of the activism associated with the Stonewall riots and gay liberation. Many gay liberationists and lesbian feminists realized that knowledge was a form of power and that ignorance reinforced oppression. Part of the activism of the 1970s was an effort to produce new knowledge by and for the community, which resulted in the research and writing of queer history.

Today, images of LGBT people are almost everywhere in popular culture. One easily encounters personalities such as Ellen DeGeneres, Adam Lambert, Ricky Martin, Rosie O'Donnell, and RuPaul, or television series such as *Glee* and *Modern Family*. But everyday life and culture in the United States looked very different in the decade before Stonewall. The new breed of young, militant activists condemned the silence that enshrouded queer lives and blocked open discussion of same-sex love and life. They conducted frequent protests against invisibility in the media and popular culture. They deplored the ways that this silence and invisibility fostered profound isolation, forcing individuals to discover their sexual or gender identities alone and in shame.

Overall, activists shared a sense that generations of silence, invisibility, and isolation had made queer folk a people without a history. To the degree that there was a queer history, it was inevitably one of misery, oppression, and suffering; the farther back in time one went, the more dismal the stories would be. Yet, among those activists in the 1970s were a few women and men who decided that their contribution to this new liberation project would be to help break the silence, shatter the invisibility, and end the isolation by uncovering a hidden history of same-sex-loving and gender-crossing people. As individuals and as members of community-based history projects, they began excavating a queer past.[1]

What did this first generation of historians discover? Let me offer four examples.

Eric Garber wrote about Harlem in the 1920s and 1930s. He looked at the literary, cultural, and entertainment circles that flourished there in the 1920s in the wake of the Great Migration of African Americans to northern cities. Among the writers, artists, and performers of the Harlem Renaissance, Garber found evidence of men-loving men and women-loving women. He used the figure of Bruce Nugent, a young visual artist and writer, to suggest the extensive social networks that existed among these figures. Using songs such as "Sissy Man" as examples, Garber described the ways in which the blues music of the era openly addressed homosexual themes. He discovered that male and female impersonation was an important feature of Harlem nightlife. For instance, Gladys Bentley, who performed in tuxedo and top hat, was a popular entertainer. Garber's work proclaimed that, two generations before Stonewall and gay liberation, there was nothing hidden, silent, or invisible about Harlem's queer life.[2]

Elizabeth Kennedy and Madeline Davis wrote the history of a different pre-Stonewall community. In *Boots of Leather, Slippers of Gold*, they moved away from the nation's biggest metropolis and zoomed in on Buffalo, New York. They investigated the world that working-class lesbians, both white and black, created there between the 1930s and 1960s. Through oral histories, Kennedy and Davis were able to reconstruct elaborate social networks. They uncovered circles of friendship and romance that were centered in private house parties and the commercialized space of bars. The gender-crossing clothing and carriage of butch women acted like a magnet, drawing others to them and building community around them. These lesbians fought–literally–for the right to claim public space, to hold their girlfriends' hands, and to dance in a bar. They fought heterosexual men who invaded their spaces and police who tried to arrest them. Kennedy and Davis found that, between 1930 and 1970, a more stable, extensive, and visible lesbian world coalesced in Buffalo.[3]

Allan Berube added another significant piece to our knowledge of a queer past. Berube was a founder of the San Francisco Lesbian and Gay History Project and, in the late 1970s and early 1980s, composed several illustrated lectures on local queer history. Through a friend of a friend, he learned of a cache of letters exchanged between gay GIs during World War II. The discovery launched him on a path that led eventually to his book *Coming Out under Fire: The History of Gay Men and Women during World War II.*[4]

In Berube's telling, the war years proved decisive in forging a collective lesbian and gay identity and building urban communities. The war took many

97

millions of young men and women out of their small towns and family environments; it put them in same-sex environments. For men, this mostly meant the military; for women, it predominantly consisted of working in civilian jobs and living in boarding houses in cities where the young male population had evaporated. It gave lots of young adults who were so inclined the freedom to experience same-sex love away from the usual constraints. And, at the end of the war, they did not all go back home. Many stayed in the cities to which they had migrated or had spent their leave. They helped to create in the postwar decade a new urban gay and lesbian world.

The last example comes from my own work. I went looking for a pre-Stonewall history of activism. I found that, in the early days of the Cold War and its anticommunist witch hunts, some lesbians, gay men, and bisexuals decided to resist the intensifying oppression by banding together to fight back. They created organizations like the Mattachine Society and the Daughters of Bilitis, which had chapters in several cities. Because visibility carried risks, they worked cautiously. They often used pseudonyms to protect themselves. But they published magazines that broke the media's silence. They won allies in the churches and among doctors and lawyers. They picketed in Washington, D.C., against the federal government's discriminatory policies. They gave interviews to the media. They developed slogans like "gay is good" and "gay power" before Stonewall. Their work was not earthshaking. It wasn't as dramatic and far-reaching as what gay liberationists and lesbian feminists did in the 1970s. But they laid some groundwork and floated new ideas. Theirs was a form of organized, self-conscious resistance.[5]

These examples cover lots of ground, stretching across five decades. They consider whites and blacks, men and women, working-class and middle-class people, social and cultural life, and public advocacy and political organizing. Yet these examples, as well as others I have not mentioned, also have some things in common. They are stories of visibility before Stonewall and gay liberation. They are stories of people breaking the silence. They are stories of people finding one another and building community.

The first generation of queer historical writing demonstrates two overarching themes. Almost without exception these studies are stories of resistance. Whether singing songs on stage or strutting on the street, whether risking arrest on Saturday night by going to a bar or refusing to return to your small town after being discharged from the military, these histories all describe resistance. The writers do not erase oppression. In fact, most agree that the decades after

World War II were particularly harsh, full of open attacks on homosexuality. But this is not a one-sided story of oppression. Instead, resistance is a key element.

These works are also thoroughly "queer-centered." By this I mean that, in all of these histories, the key actors and movers are gay men, lesbians, and gender-crossers. Their initiative, their decisions, and their choices make history. The compelling story we told was one in which queer folks make worlds of their own and shape their own destinies. To appropriate the title of a book on women's history, they were "heroes of their own lives."

It is not surprising that this is what we found. The first substantial body of work on LGBT history was researched, written, and published between the mid-1970s and mid-1990s. All of us who produced these studies either came of age in the 1960s and 1970s or were deeply affected by these decades. It was a time of massive social movements for justice. Resistance was the order of the day, and it was led by people–African Americans, Chicanos, women–as part of a larger effort to build a collective identity. The truthfulness and the plausibility of the history we wrote emerged from what we knew and saw around us. Our interpretations were enabled by the world of social movements and community resistance that gave birth to our work. When we looked around, we saw ordinary people making their own history and shaping their own destiny. We did our research and that is what we found too.

Now let me jump forward from that earlier generation of historical writing and describe some of what I am uncovering in my Chicago research. At first glance, much of it is thoroughly consistent with the content and interpretive framework that I have just sketched out. For instance, Chicago's South Side in the 1920s and 1930s parallels the Harlem experience described by Eric Garber. Blues artists such as Alberta Hunter, Ethel Waters, Bessie Smith and, especially, Ma Rainey, had a strong presence in Chicago. The *Chicago Defender* promoted their careers and celebrated their achievements. Hunter, Rainey, Smith, and Waters all had romantic or sexual relationships with women. Rainey was arrested and spent a night in jail after police busted a late night party of women in various states of undress.[6]

Angela Davis has written persuasively about these blues singers, arguing that one of the distinguishing features of their music is the "pervasive sexual imagery." The sexuality expressed by them was not just what, in our time, we describe as heterosexual. "Prove It on Me Blues," a song composed by Rainey and recorded in 1928, has these lyrics:

Went out last night with a crowd of my friends
They must've been women, 'cause I don't like no men . . .
Wear my clothes just like any old man
'Cause they say I do it, ain't nobody caught me
Sure got to prove it on me.

The ad that ran in the *Chicago Defender* to promote the record pictures Rainey as a burly figure in shirt, tie, and a man's tailored jacket, picking up two dolled-up femmes.[7]

The male analogue of these blues singers was the female impersonator. The *Chicago Defender*, the primary newspaper in the African-American community and one with national reach, enthusiastically promoted female impersonators. It followed the careers of some of them, including Dick Barrow and Walter Winston, who had strong Chicago ties. It heaped compliments on shows put together by Miss Valda Gray, a leading impresario of the genre, and praised the performers at the Cabin Inn, a South Side establishment, as "America's most outstanding female impersonators."[8] During the 1936 Christmas season, the *Chicago Defender* sponsored a major benefit to help needy families. Seven thousand attended, and thousands more were turned away. The show brought together a galaxy of stars, including such a luminary as Louis Armstrong. Valda Gray was there, along with her troupe of impersonators. When the newspaper reported on the benefit the day after Christmas, it featured photographs of "Doris" and "Peaches" and "Dixie" and "Petite," all dressed in their glamorous best.[9]

Like other big cities, and confirming the interpretation of Berube, post-World War II Chicago had a dense concentration of bars and clubs that catered to gay men, lesbians, and gender crossers and that helped build community and solidarity. From the 1940s through the 1960s, a variety of popular nightspots—among them the Windup, the Fun Lounge, the Front Page, the Hollywood Bowl, the Carousel, the Annex, Sam's, the Baton, the Trip, and the Chesterfield—drew huge crowds. Clubs could be found on the South and West sides, but the densest concentration was in neighborhoods just north of the city's downtown business district.

Chicago's experience also confirms a picture of the 1950s and 1960s as intensely oppressive decades, what I describe to my undergraduates as "the worst time to be queer." In scores of articles over a three-year period, including some on the front page, the *Chicago Tribune* gave prominent coverage to the

100

McCarthy-era witch hunts by the federal government. Reporters commonly described gay men with phrases such as "moral degenerates," "unmentionables," "nests of perverts," and "men of depraved tendencies."[10]

In a climate of such overt hostility, Chicago police felt free to harass anyone who seemed gay or lesbian. Gender crossers of either sex were especially vulnerable. City law prohibited wearing clothing for the purpose of concealing one's sex. Women with short hair who wore pants with the zipper in the front could be—and were—arrested. One woman remembered the humiliation of sitting at a bar during a police raid and having an officer shine a flashlight at her crotch to make sure she was wearing woman's slacks.[11] In November 1970, two police detectives fired multiple shots into the back of James Clay, a black drag queen who was trying to avoid arrest.[12] Men sitting in parks known to be cruising areas were arrested for loitering. Handsome young cops dressed in street clothes staked out parks, alleys, and public toilets, soliciting the men they encountered for sex. Men who responded were arrested for solicitation.

Above all, Chicago police targeted gay and lesbian bars. They felt free to harass businesses and their patrons with impunity. They might park their cars outside a bar and simply sit there, an effective way of keeping fearful customers from entering. Or, they might enter and casually look around. Business would then evaporate because, in the words of one manager, "everybody would walk out."[13] More ominously, plainclothes officers might enter unannounced and unseen. If they noticed any physical contact—an arm around a waist, a couple holding hands, a simple kiss—they could arrest the manager and employees for maintaining a disorderly house, charge the offending patrons with public lewdness, and cart off the other customers as patrons of a disorderly house.

Throughout these decades, bar raids were a fact of life, a danger every patron risked by walking through the door. Most raids escaped broader public notice but, periodically, especially in the case of mass arrests, city newspapers reported the events. In 1949, police arrested 87 at the Windup, on State Street near Chicago Avenue. In 1951, they arrested 58 at Cyrano's Tavern, at Division and State Streets. In 1962, police hauled away 40 from the Front Page on Rush Street.[14] The most notorious raid occurred in 1964 at The Fun Lounge, a place just outside the city limits. Playing upon fears about corrupting youth, the front-page headline in the Sunday *Chicago Sun-Times* announced "Area Teachers among 109 Seized in Raid on Vice Den." Over the next days, newspapers in the city carried the names and addresses of public employees picked up in the raid and tracked the termination of their employment.[15] Newspaper coverage of

101

raids served as an insidious labeling device. It alerted readers to the deviants in their midst and told queer folks of the dangers of visiting gay bars.

Under these circumstances, bar owners quickly learned that they needed to make payoffs to the police to stay open. Yet even bribes did not guarantee freedom from police harassment. One tavern owner described his relationship to law enforcement this way: "I felt like I had the sword of Damocles over my head."[16] Such conditions meant that few legitimate entrepreneurs invested in gay or lesbian bars. Instead, bars were often operated by individuals with ties to organized crime. Since owners expected to be shut after a certain amount of time, they tried to secure quick profits. Watered-down drinks, high prices, and dingy atmospheres were the norm. One patron perfectly captured the paradox of bar life in this era. "The bars are the only place for gay people to go to get together outside of home," he said. "There is no question that they were for shit."

Chicago also resembled other large cities in that, by the 1960s, signs of organized resistance by lesbians and gay men were growing. The city had chapters of the Daughters of Bilitis and the Mattachine Society, the two main national homophile organizations. Mattachine especially railed against Chicago police, accusing them of "entrapment, shakedowns, brutality, and corruption." Late in 1966, homophile activists in the city were so enraged that they adopted a formulation of black activists and raised a call for "gay power." To my knowledge, this was the first such use of the term anywhere. [17]

The gay liberation movement that the Stonewall rebellion helped provoke came to Chicago very early. A group naming itself Chicago Gay Liberation started meeting on the South Side, in Hyde Park, before the end of 1969. Chicago was one of only three cities to hold a rally and march in June 1970 to commemorate the first anniversary of Stonewall. *Lavender Woman*, one of the earliest lesbian feminist newspapers, began publishing in Chicago in 1971. African American and Latino activists formed an organization named "Third World Gay Revolution." Over the next years, lesbian, gay, and transgender activists demonstrated against businesses that harassed or discriminated against queer clientele. They picketed newspapers that published derogatory articles. They demonstrated outside police district offices to protest harassment. They held rallies in places known to be cruising areas, as if daring the police to arrest them.[18]

By the mid-1970s, after only a few years of high-spirited militancy by these groups, police harassment, especially of bars, plummeted. It did not stop entirely, but it became sporadic and occasional rather than systemic and pervasive. The implications of this shift cannot be overstated. The decline in harassment brought immediate, dramatic, and visible changes. By the second half of the 1970s, one could point not merely to an increase in the number of bars owned by gay entrepreneurs but also to greater longevity for these businesses, more geographic concentration, a relaxed queer presence on the streets, and the coalescence of a neighborhood that was, increasingly, described as gay.

It is fair to say that what I just described about Chicago sounds very much like the old plot line of gay and lesbian history: a queer-centric story of resistance in which lesbians, gay men, and gender crossers band together to resist oppression while building community in the process. As we move into and through the 1970s, silence, invisibility, and isolation fade away as appropriate descriptors. Yet the resistance of queer Chicagoans, whether through organizations and formal mobilizations or through spontaneous protest actions, does not explain a vital part of this story—the end of systematic police harassment of gay bars and the opportunity it provided for a flourishing gay neighborhood to emerge. How can we explain it?

The harassment of bars was one tiny element in a much larger story of bribery and corruption, police and organized crime, and the day-to-day operations of the political machine of Mayor Richard J. Daley and the Cook County Democratic party. In the huge literature on Daley and the Democratic machine over which he presided, certain characterizations recur. The journalist Mike Royko, no friend of the mayor, called Daley, in the 1960s, "with the single exception of the president, the most powerful politician in the country." The authors of the most applauded biography of Daley described him as "the most powerful local politician America has ever produced."[19]

103

The heart of the mayor's power was the political machine and the patronage which he dispensed to its members. Daley reputedly knew many of the Democratic precinct captains by name. According to biographers Cohen and Taylor, in the 1960s he had close to 40,000 patronage jobs. City employment demanded loyalty to the machine and its candidates, from mobilizing voters at election time to favoring important supporters of the machine. In return, city employees could expect a certain amount of freedom in performing their duties, including the freedom to obtain supplements to their salaries. Whether they were building inspectors or property assessors, machine loyalists in city jobs knew that they could get away with a lot.

For police working in districts that housed the city's nightlife, including the main concentration of gay bars, this meant payoffs from tavern owners. The

Chicago Tribune described the practice as "so deeply entrenched as to be considered a way of life—a license to steal, graft a part of the emoluments of the job."[20] The web of corruption was so tight that city officials whose job it was to investigate corruption surrounding liquor licenses—for instance, an assistant state attorney and an assistant corporate counsel who handled liquor license revocations—were themselves either the owner of a gay bar or the lawyer for a gay bar.[21]

In a system like this, a few hundred gay and lesbian liberationist hippies demonstrating outside a police district office had no capacity to modify practices toward gay bars. To stop the extortion and harassment required piercing the power of the machine. Ending the raids on gay bars and the arrests of patrons required challenging the ability of city employees loyal to the machine to reap an expected benefit of their job.

What then broke the back of pervasive harassment and, as a consequence, opened the way for a visible gay neighborhood to take shape? To put it most baldly: the election of Richard Nixon as president in 1968.

As long as a Democrat occupied the White House, there was unlikely to be any serious investigation of corruption in Chicago. Daley had received credit for delivering the presidency to John Kennedy in 1960. Lyndon Johnson consulted with Daley before shaping major legislative proposals that might impact urban politics, such as his War on Poverty. In 1967, Johnson and congressional Democrats honored Daley as "Democrat of the Year."[22] The power of the political machine was such that Daley's protégés were elected as state's attorneys in Illinois and hence were unlikely to investigate corruption. Daley's influence with Democratic presidents meant that machine loyalists received appointment as U.S. attorney for northern Illinois, thus closing another route to exposing malfeasance. By contrast, a Republican president, especially one like Nixon who attributed his 1960 defeat to Daley's machine, would be eager to do what no Democratic president would have allowed: investigate corruption in Chicago.

A sign of what this shift in investigatory power meant came early in 1970 when the U.S. attorney impaneled a grand jury to investigate prosecutorial and police misdeeds in the December 1969 killings of Fred Hampton and Mark Clark, two Chicago Black Panther Party leaders. If the idea of Richard Nixon and John Mitchell, his attorney general, supporting justice for black militants seems to stretch credibility, then one can appreciate how intent the new administration was on discrediting Daley and undermining his power. In spring

1970, the grand jury completed its investigation and issued a scathing 243-page report that laid the groundwork for later indictments of thirteen police officers and Edward Hanrahan, a Daley protégé who was Cook County state attorney. The U.S. attorney's office released the report on the mayor's birthday.[23] In September 1972, James Thompson, the U.S. attorney in northern Illinois who later became the Republican governor, handed down indictments of more than six dozen Democratic Party workers for voter fraud in primaries held earlier in the year.[24]

In 1969, the year Nixon took office, a seemingly random case of a tavern shakedown by the police surfaced. Bob Weidrich, a columnist for the *Chicago Tribune,* began to write about it, and his coverage provided the trigger for an FBI inquiry. In February 1971, U.S. attorney Thompson impaneled another grand jury to investigate the extortion of bar owners. For twenty-two months it gathered evidence, including testimony from gay bar owners who were promised immunity. The grand jury uncovered a "police extortion racket" that "preyed on tavern owners in the Rush Street and Old Town nightlife strips, extracting monthly tribute from them."[25] Between 1972 and 1974 fifty-six police officers, including the captain of the Chicago Avenue district, which contained the largest concentration of gay bars in the city, were indicted on corruption charges. The investigation, indictments, and trials produced hundreds of news stories in the press, from late 1972 to early 1974. Headlines that stretched across the front page recall the sensationalism of earlier ones about raids on gay bars, while the language used—a "sordid spectacle" wrote one *Chicago Sun-Times* reporter—echoed the Lavender Scare of the 1950s.[26]

105

The main trial of officers from the Chicago Avenue district began in August 1973 and lasted six weeks. It generated a trial transcript almost 7,700 pages long. Fifty-five bar owners and managers, including from many of the city's gay bars, testified.[27] When the trial was over, thirty-four officers were found guilty, and hundreds more were transferred. The scandal forced the resignation of James Conlisk, the police superintendent, whose father was a close friend of Mayor Daley.[28]

After almost two years of unrelenting exposure of police malfeasance, it was no longer possible for the police to harass gay bars and intimidate their patrons. True, an especially homophobic officer might target an individual or a particular business, or a district commander might go after a bar because of rumors about drug dealing or other irregularities. But the investigations, indictments, trials, and convictions of police officers and commanders in these years broke the back forever of systematic harassment of bars. That in turn allowed for the flowering of a new kind of gay entrepreneurship and the growth for the first time of an openly queer neighborhood. This may be the single most profound change in the post-Stonewall decade, yet queer activism and resistance had little to do with it.

What are the implications of a conclusion like this? Does it mean that the earlier work some of us did—putting lesbians, gay men, and transgender people at the center of their own history and crediting self-conscious resistance as propelling this history forward—is no longer sustainable? Does it mean that I am about to start writing a new history from the top down, one in which big forces beyond the control of ordinary people rather than social movements built from the bottom up shape change?

I don't think so. But I know that part of what allows me to see Chicago's queer history in this way is the experience, different from the 1960s and 1970s, of having lived through more than a quarter century of the Reagan/Bush world. In areas as diverse as tax policy, banking regulation, and sex education, top-down decision making has driven events. Instead, my hope is that by embedding local queer stories in a larger political economy, a larger national political history, they will become less separated and self-contained, less ghettoized inside a lavender bubble, and be seen rather as more integral and connected to broader narratives of U.S. history.

ENDNOTES

1. Key early works include Jonathan Ned Katz, *Gay American History: Lesbians and Gay Men in the U.S.A.* (New York: Thomas Crowell, 1976); Lillian Faderman, *Surpassing the Love of Men: Romantic Friendship and Love between Women from the Renaissance to the Present* (New York: William Morrow and Company, 1981); and the special issue of *Radical History Review* (Spring-Summer 1979).

2. Eric Garber, "A Spectacle in Color: The Lesbian and Gay Subculture of Jazz Age Harlem," in Martin Duberman, Martha Vicinus, and George Chauncey, Jr., *Hidden from History: Reclaiming the Gay and Lesbian Past* (New York: New American Library, 1989), 318–31.

3. Elizabeth Lapovsky Kennedy and Madeline D. Davis, *Boots of Leather, Slippers of Gold: The History of a Lesbian Community* (New York: Routledge, 1993).

4. Allan Berube, *Coming Out Under Fire: The History of Gay Men and Women in World War Two* (New York: Free Press, 1990). Berube's essays on both World War II and community history have been collected in *My Desire for History: Essays in Gay, Community, and Labor History* (Chapel Hill: University of North Carolina Press, 2011).

5. John D'Emilio, *Sexual Politics, Sexual Communities: The Making of a Homosexual Minority in the United States, 1940-1970* (Chicago: University of Chicago Press, 1983; 2nd edition, 1998).

6. On the careers of these performers, see Chris Albertson, *Bessie* (New Haven: Yale University Press, 2003); Stephen Bourne, *Ethel Waters: Stormy Weather* (Lanham, Md.: Scarecrow Press, 2007); Sandra Lieb, *Mother of the Blues: A Study of Ma Rainey* (Amherst: University of Massachusetts Press, 1981); Frank C. Taylor, *Alberta Hunter: A Celebration in Blues* (New York: McGraw Hill, 1987).

7. Angela Y. Davis, *Blues Legacies and Black Feminism* (New York: Vintage Paperback, 1999), 3-4, 8, 238; *Chicago Defender*, September 22, 1928: 7

8. *Chicago Defender*, October 22, 1938: 19.

9. *Chicago Defender*, December 26, 1936: 3, 20.

10. For examples of the language used, see *Chicago Tribune*, March 26, 1950: 5; March 30, 1950: 1; July 27, 1950: 14; and October 5, 1951: 15.

11. Interview with Agnes Hassett, June 6, 1995, Jack Rinella Papers, Box 2, Gerber/Hart Library, Chicago.

12. On the killing of James Clay, see *Chicago Defender*, November 28, 1970: 1, and *Chicago Sun-Times*, November 26, 1970: 46.

13. *Chicago Tribune,* August 31, 1973: 1.

14. On these bar raids, see *Chicago Tribune*, January 10, 1949: 1; January 22, 1949: 9; February 5, 1949: 4; December 31, 1951: B7; and March 27, 1962: B5.

15. *Chicago Sunday Sun-Times*, April 26, 1964: 1, and *Chicago's Sunday American*, April 26, 1964: 1.

16. *Chicago Tribune*, August 16, 1973: 2.

17. *Mattachine Midwest Newsletter*, December 1966: 3 (copy in Gerber/Hart Library).

18. Accounts of activism in the early 1970s can be found in *Chicago Gay Liberation Newsletter* and *Chicago Gay Alliance Newsletter*, both in Gerber/Hart Library.

19. Mike Royko, *Boss: Richard J. Daley of Chicago* (New York: Plume Books, 1988), 125; Adam Cohen and Elizabeth Taylor, *American Pharaoh Mayor Richard J. Daley, His Battle for Chicago and the Nation* (New York: Little Brown, 2000), 7.

20. *Chicago Tribune*, May 14, 1972: 1.

21. *Chicago Tribune*, August 16, 1973: 2.

22. *Chicago Tribune*, May 10, 1967: 1.

23. *Chicago Defender*, January 5, 1970: 1, 3; and *Chicago Tribune*, May 16, 1970: W2, W6; *Chicago Defender*, August 25, 1971: 1–2; and *Chicago Tribune*, August 25, 1971: 1, 12.

24. *Chicago Tribune*, October 28, 1972: 1.

25. *Chicago Tribune*, November 22, 1972: 5; December 31, 1972: 1.

26. *Chicago Sun-Times*, December 29, 1972: 1.

27. *U.S. v. Braasch, 505 F. 2d 139.*

28. *Chicago Tribune*, October 11, 1973: 6.

GAYS AND GOSPEL
A Queer History of Sacred Music

By E. Patrick Johnson

Gospel music has always played an integral role in African American culture. Indeed, gospel music—alongside spirituals and blues—has been heralded as the music of a people who have overcome trials and tribulations, heartaches and strife, social and political struggle. Gospel music is that hand clapping, foot stomping, body rocking, hand waving, choir swaying, Sunday morning/moaning, jump joy for Jesus shouting, transforming, spirit moving, awe inspiring, cultural art form that led the downtrodden and the weary, the sick and the afflicted, the shut in and the shut out, the "closed in the right mind," to believe that soon and very soon I will be done with the troubles of the world, because when they was way down yonder by themselves and couldn't hear nobody pray, they knew that if God delivered Daniel, if God delivered Shadrach, Meshach and Abednego, then surely, surely, surely, He will deliver me.

Chicago is the birthplace of what we now know as contemporary gospel music. Arizona Dranes, a blind pianist from Dallas, Texas, is credited with creating in the 1920s what became known as the "gospel beat," which emphasized a heavy accent on the first beat in musical units of two beats and on two and four in musical units of four. The term *gospel music,* however, was first used by Thomas Dorsey (1899–1993) in 1921 to describe his first written song, "If I Don't Get There," which he composed at the Pilgrim Baptist Church located on the 3300 block of Indiana Avenue. Dorsey became known as the Father of Gospel Music, and his most famous song is "Precious Lord."

One of the controversies surrounding the advent of gospel music is its connection to other secular forms such as blues and jazz. Dorsey himself was a blues musician who played blues and jazz on Saturday night and sacred music on

Figure 1. Thomas Dorsey (at piano) with Ma Rainey's band.

Sunday morning (fig. 1). Even after he had given up playing the blues, his gospel compositions reflected the imagery and rhythms of the blues. Despite the objections of many of the "saints" in the church, gospel music took hold because it arose during the Great Depression, when worldly troubles were not easily soothed by traditional hymns and spirituals. According to Dorsey, "I wrote to give them something to lift them out of that Depression. They could sing at church but the singing had no life, no spirit."[1] Thus, the blurring of the secular and the sacred was inevitable, and with that melding, gospel provided a space for those who were not necessarily accepted around the "welcome table"— namely sexual and gender nonconformists—to participate in the musical form's continued growth and innovation. From its built-in theatricality and bluesy beats to its suggestive lyrics, gospel thus became a vehicle for the expression of more than just spirituality.

This essay highlights key figures of the LGBT community who have played a significant role in the history of gospel music. Because of the silence around sexuality in the church in general and homosexuality in particular, many of the figures I discuss never confirmed or denied their sexuality; rather, speculation, hearsay, and oral histories of those who were close to them or alleged lovers form the basis of their categorization as queer. As Gayle Wald writes: "Notwithstanding the question of their truth, rumors contain meaning, especially in the insular world of mid-century gospel. Like other artistic realms, the gospel circuit had its own protocols of private and public behavior, of what could be said out loud and what could only be whispered about or not said at all."[2] I also share my own and others' stories of growing up in the church choir as what I call "church sissies," who used the choir to affirm our budding homosexuality. Finally, I discuss some of the aesthetics of gospel that make queer performance possible.

The great migration of southern blacks to Chicago in the 1930s and 1940s made Chicago a central hub for the creation and dissemination of gospel music. The city was rich with musicians who played both secular and sacred music. The abundance of musicians and singers in Chicago, especially blues and jazz performers, made it an attractive stop for musicians traveling across the country, some of whom made the city home. One such musician was guitar-playing Sister Rosetta Tharpe (1915–73), a gospel artist whose music constantly straddled the line between the secular and the sacred (fig. 2). Garnering most of her popularity in the 1930s and 1940s, Tharpe combined the sacred vocals of her church background with jazz and blues-guitar, recording many songs with (homo)sexual undertones. For example, Tharpe recorded Thomas Dorsey's "Hide Me in Thy Bosom," which she also recorded as "Rock Me" under the Decca label. Because God or Jesus is never referenced in the song, the lyrics remain suggestive: "Hide me in thy bosom till the storm of life is over/Rock me in the cradle of thy love." Rosetta's handling of her guitar and the double entendre of the lyrics only buttressed rumors about her lesbian dalliances, especially with "Madame" Marie Knight, a sanctified singer from New Jersey with whom Tharpe recorded several songs. While I cannot detect whether he is signifying or not, gospel music historian Clarence Boyer's description of the duet speaks volumes:

> Their most outstanding recording was "Up above My Head" from a November 1947 session in which Tharpe provides the call and Knight the response. Although Knight's voice is darker than Tharpe's, they made the perfect gospel duet, even on the chorus after Tharpe's solo interlude where Knight *assumes the role of the male bass* from gospel quartets, essaying her range from the *top to the bottom*.[3]

111

Figure 2. Rosetta Tharpe and Marie Knight. Michael Ochs Archive/Getty Images.

Figure 3. Chicago's Pilgrim Baptist Church, c. 1945. Library of Congress.

While Knight denied the rumors about her and Tharpe, many of those closest to Tharpe suggested that not only was she intimate with Knight but with other women as well, even while she was married. Whatever the case, it is clear that Sister Rosetta Tharpe's unconventional style—onstage and off—queered gospel music of the era and perhaps offered other "possibilities of intimacy in a world where lines of gender and sexuality were religiously policed."[4]

Chicago is also the birthplace of one of the most famous gay pioneers of gospel music, Reverend James Cleveland (1931–91), known as the Crown Prince of gospel. Anyone listening to Cleveland's records today would never guess that he had ever been a boy soprano. As a member of the children's choir under the direction of Thomas Dorsey at Pilgrim Baptist Church (fig. 3), Cleveland sang solo on many songs and began studying piano at age five. As a teenager he joined a local group, the Thorne Crusaders, with whom he sang for eight years. The combination of a lower register brought on by puberty and vocal strain from singing with the Thorne Crusaders left him with the "gruff, unpretty voice" that made it so distinctive. [5]

Over his more than forty-year career, Cleveland worked with some of the greatest gospel singers and musicians in the country, many of whom were both mentors and protégés. These include Roberta Martin and Albertina Walker for whom he served as a composer, arranger, pianist, and occasional singer/narrator for her group the Caravans. Walker provided Cleveland with the opportunity to make his very first recording after convincing her record company to record him. He quit and returned to the Caravans a number of times to join other groups. His recording of "Peace Be Still," an obscure eighteenth-century madrigal, sold hundreds of thousands of copies thanks to Cleveland's comforting growl and emotional command.

Cleveland founded his own choir, the Southern California Community Choir, as well as a church, Cornerstone Institutional Baptist Church, in Los Angeles that, at the time of his death, boasted more than seven thousand members. Indeed, Cleveland's work with choirs is what has made his legacy so enduring. In his vocal arrangements, he removed the bass part, creating three-part harmony instead of four. This is one of the reasons the tenor part in many gospel compositions is so unforgiving on the male voice (no doubt influenced by his own strained voice as a child), often requiring tenors to hit and sustain G, A flat, and even B flat above middle C. But the choir was also a space where, as I discuss later, gay men could show off their vocal virtuosity. Cleveland recorded most of his songs live and loved the vamp (the repetition of a line), and the songs he wrote spoke of everyday trials and tribulations of being black in America.

His most enduring legacy, however, is the Gospel Music Workshop of America (GMWA), a convention that he organized in 1968 and that continues today. GMWA has more than thirty-thousand members in 150 chapters and has produced some of the world's most popular contemporary gospel singers and musicians, such as John P. Kee and Kirk Franklin. The GMWA is also widely known as a place where queers in the gospel scene cruise and party, which is why in some circles it is referred to as "Gay Men and Women of America." Cleveland himself is rumored to have had a penchant for his younger male protégés who were constantly around him during the convention. Like the church itself, it was not uncommon for queer singers and musicians to use the occasion of a "holy" conference for secular purposes. Even the National Baptist Convention provided a site for queer desire to spring eternal. In her autobiography, Willa Ward-Royster, sister to famous gospel great Clara Ward (fig. 4) described how her sister was outed at a convention gathering:

Figure 4. Clara Ward. Michael Ochs Archive/Getty Images.

We had met plenty of gays and usually had great fun in their company—it was easy enough to admire their creativity and wit—but I couldn't for the life of me understand why Clara and I had been invited to such a party.

I soon got my explanation when one of the young men we had come with bounced down the stairs in a T-shirt and a towel, on his way to get some ice. In passing he excused himself for not entertaining us but offered, "Honey, I'm on a mission. When Mother gets back upstairs, she's gone dive right in the middle of all that flesh. Clara, if I'd have thought about it, I would have invited someone for you. I know this sharp young child who'd just love you, she's a Stone man, Honey." The guy probably thought I knew, but until then, I had no idea that my sister had dabbled in homosexual activities. She was really embarrassed that I had heard, and we were both so uncomfortable that we left.[6]

116

While we must take Willa's story at face value since Clara is deceased, rumor and willful silences are some of the only ways in which we can document homosexuality within these communities. Historian John Howard calls recollections such as Willa's "twice-told stories." He wrote: "This hearsay evidence— inadmissable in court, unacceptable to some historians—is essential to the recuperation of queer histories. The age-old squelching of our words and desires can be replicated over time when we adhere to ill-suited and unbending standards of historical methodology."[7] Relying on hearsay and rumor to document homosexuality in the gospel world is particularly important since keeping one's sexuality a secret would have been critical not only to one's livelihood but also to one's acceptance in the church.

Cleveland passed away in 1991 in Los Angeles. Although an official statement declared that he died of natural causes, many in the black LGBT community knew that Cleveland died of complications due to AIDS. Not until months after his death, when his foster son and alleged lover Christopher Harris filed a patrimony suit against his estate, did folks began to wonder if Cleveland was the man they thought they knew. In fact, probably most of his church and choir members knew about his sexuality, but chose to overlook it or deny it altogether. This willful denial speaks to the investment that many black communities have in perceptions of those outside the race. As Gayle Wald puts it:

Homosexuality ranked as a different order of sin . . . reflecting broader social and cultural prohibitions on sexual identities that violated . . . the natural, God-given order of things. For many black people, homosexuality threatened to hinder the progress of "the race" as a whole, insofar as they believed progress to be predicated on mainstream acceptance.[8]

This investment in respectability manifests in what I believe to be an unholy trinity: shame, guilt, and denial. Parishioners see what they want to see, deny what they do not want to see, or feel shame or guilt about what is hidden in plain sight. This is a blessing and curse for queer singers and musicians who are at once ostracized for being an "abomination" but also celebrated for their gifts and talents. The latter does provide some leeway for gender nonconformity in the name of the Holy Spirit. How else could one explain the number of flamboyant singers such as Little Richard, who grew up in and returned to the church, whose sexuality seems to have never been an issue? The same can be said of gender nonconformity. An example is Willmer "Little Ax" Broadnax (1916–94), who was one of the great post-war gospel quartet singers. Broadnax was a diminutive man with a big voice. He and his brother, William "Big Ax," were born in Houston and formed a quartet called the Golden Echoes in Southern California. William eventually left for Atlanta, where he joined the Five Trumpets, but Willmer stayed on as lead singer. In 1950, Willmer joined the Spirit of Memphis Quartet, one of the best gospel quartets to ever record. Although his time with the quartet lasted only two years, he went on to perform with other great groups like the Fairfield Four and the Five Blind Boys of Mississippi, with whom he recorded into the 1970s and 1980s. Upon his death in 1994, it was discovered that "he" was indeed a "she," who had been passing all of "her" life.[9]

117

Not all queer gospel singers led hidden or clandestine lives, however. Sylvester, the high priestess drag queen of the 1970s disco era, started singing at Palm Lane, which was a member of the Church of God in Christ (COGIC). Born in 1944, Sylvester James, known as "Dooni" as a child, grew up in South Central Los Angeles.[10] Known for singing in falsetto (despite a rich baritone voice), Sylvester's music is undeniably tinged with the gospel music he sang as a child, especially on songs such as "You Make Me Feel (Mighty Real)," which became a disco anthem and maintains the 4/4 rhythm that gospel is known for. Although Sylvester was celebrated by secular disco fans, he was also embraced by progressive churches such as the Love Center Church in East Oakland, founded by Rev. Walter Hawkins (of "Oh Happy Day" fame). Hawkins often invited Sylvester to sing at the church, and he was sometimes accompanied by Hawkins and his brother Edwin. He also gave the eulogy at Sylvester's funeral.

One of Sylvester's friends and co-singers at the Love Center in East Oakland was the Reverend Yvette Flunder. An out lesbian and activist, Flunder is a native San Franciscan, and a third-generation preacher with roots in the Church of God in Christ. She was licensed in COGIC and later ordained by Bishop Walter Hawkins of Love Center Ministries, where she served as associate pastor and administrator. In 1984 Flunder began performing and recording with Walter Hawkins and the Family and the Love Center Choir. Flounder is also an ordained Minister of the United Church of Christ and a graduate of the Ministry Studies and Master of Arts programs at the Pacific School of Religion, Berkeley, California. She founded the City of Refuge Community Church UCC in 1991 in order to unite a gospel ministry with a social ministry. City of Refuge is a thriving inner-city congregation that celebrates the radically inclusive love of Jesus Christ. Preaching a message of action, the church has experienced steady numerical and spiritual growth and is now located in the south of Market area of San Francisco. The song for which she is most known is "Thank You," recorded in 1990 on Walter Hawkins' *Love Alive IV* album.

The lives and careers of these gospel artists—both those open about their sexuality and those not—reflect the array of queer performers and the ways in which they negotiated, reconciled, and celebrated their spirituality and sexuality. Their stories, however, are not unique. Many of us "church sissies" and "church butches," who have not become famous for our singing but were raised in the church choir, have similar stories. Some of these experiences have been captured in oral histories and in literature. It takes rumor, hearsay, oral history, and fiction to capture the fullness of the history of gospel. As someone reared in the church and in the church choir, I share my own personal story of growing up in the church choir.

My mother dragged me to church every Sunday. Like most of the folk in my community in rural western North Carolina, we were Baptists. I remember the first time I saw someone "get happy." It scared me to death. And because I was an inquisitive child, I would often ask my mother why people were jerking their bodies, waving their hands, and dancing in the church. Without looking down at me she would pat me on the leg and say, "Shhh. They feelin' the spirit." Her explanation meant very little to me, but folks "felt the spirit" so often that I began to accept it as a part of church service.

I was one of several budding queens in the church, and we all learned very quickly—subconsciously or not—how to express and affirm our queerness without ever *naming* our sexuality—we knew, like the gospel group the Clark

Sisters, that "to name it is to claim it." Thus we used the choir as our sword and shield. In the children's choir we baby church sissies would flame as bright as we wanted, and it was totally acceptable. For many years, the choir was my saving grace. It was in the choir where I felt free to express myself and where I felt appreciated. By the time I was 12, I had garnered a reputation as the little fat boy with the high butt and high voice that could sing. I was the only male soprano, and I could out sing any of the girls in the soprano section. I got the church to shoutin' every Sunday by singing the solo originally sung by Yolanda Adams with the Southeastern Inspiration Choir out of Houston, Texas. The song is called "My Liberty"—how prophetic.

We had one of the best children's choirs in the area. Grown folks marveled, and some of my peers envied my soaring melismas and general vocal theatrics. What I realize now, but didn't back then, was that I was a budding diva, using the medium of gospel music to express not only my spirituality but also my sexual and gender identity. I would catch the spirit at times, especially during my solos, and step down out of the choir stand and twirl down the aisle—all the while holding a note and making sure that no one took the microphone out of my hand. The little queen in me was begging to show out, and I had a captive audience. I continued to sing soprano until, much to my chagrin, my voice changed at age 17. And Sherry Shade took over the lead to "My Liberty." Me? Bitter? Nooooooo.

My story of growing up and performing in the black church choir is similar to those in my book *Sweet Tea: Black Gay Men of the South—An Oral History*. For example, Chaz/Chastity, a pre-operative transgendered person who lives in my hometown in North Carolina and lives her life as "Chastity" Monday through Saturday and as "Chaz/Charles" on Sunday, explained that he/she and other little boys in the children's choir used catching the spirit as a guise to be flamboyant and later as a way to signify one's homosexuality:

> Oh yes. We say all the time, well she's just a big ole sissy, referring to a guy that's in the choir, or possibly the director, or you know, someone who's very flamboyant as far as the choir's movements, because in black choirs a lot of times there's a lot of . . . emotion in the song, not just in the way that the song is sung but in the way that you move to the song. . . . . So yes, even now when I'm observing some youth choirs, [I] can see the traits, especially with some little boys. Sometimes [when] I'm observing youth choirs, [I] can see the little boy that's got the tambourine. He's

119

just going on, and I mean, very much on time with the beating, and he's just more into it than the other kids; a lot of the times it's because of his artistic nature, and through time, you'll be able to see that I was right.[11]

Thus, the choir serves as a nurturing site for one's "creativity" and "artistic nature," for effeminate boys who might otherwise be ostracized outside the confines of that particular space. Indeed, as Bobby from Atlanta declared, "Where else but in the black church can a queen be a star whether she has talent or not? Baby, it ain't the army where you can be all that you can be, it's the church. Homophobic or not, church folk will give you your props." Black gay men have surmised that the church is a place to express their talents vis-à-vis the choir and other church performance venues. I want to be clear, however, that I am not calling into question the "authenticity" of the black queer's faith but rather suggesting that the manifestation of that faith in performance provides a vehicle through which one can also express queerness in covert ways. On the other hand, I would venture to say that there are some queens who are conscious about the limitless possibilities of queer expression via church performances and who exploit those possibilities for what they are worth—who actually take pleasure in pushing the boundaries of gender theatricality within the confines of the church.

120

Some of the pleasure and duplicity enjoyed by church sissies is represented best in African American literature. In much of James Baldwin's fiction, for example, he captured the tension between spirituality and sexuality, piety and worldliness, and holy rapture and sexual ecstasy. In the following scene from his novel *Go Tell It on the Mountain*, the narrator's description of the character Elisha playing the piano is significant:

At one moment, head thrown back, eyes closed, sweat standing on his brow, he sat at the piano, singing and playing; and then like a great black cat in trouble in the jungle, he stiffened and trembled, and cried out. Jesus, Jesus, Oh Lord Jesus. He struck on the piano one last, wild note, and threw up his hands, palms upward, stretched wide apart. The tambourines raced to fill the vacuum left by his silent piano, and his cry drew answering cries. Then he was on his feet, turning, blind, his face congested, contorted with this rage, and the muscles leaping and swelling in his long, dark neck. It seemed that he could not breathe, that his body could not contain this passion, that he would be, before their eyes, dispersed into the waiting air. His hands, rigid to the very fingertips, moved outward back against his hips, his sightless eyes looked upward, and he began to dance. Then his hands closed into fists, and his head snapped downward, his sweat loosening the grease that slicked down his hair; and the rhythm of all the others quickened to match Elisha's rhythm; his thighs moved terribly against the cloth of his suit, his heels beat on the floor, and his fists moved beside his body as though he was beating his own drum. And so, for a while, in the center of the dancers, head down, fists beating, on, on, unbearably, until it seemed the walls of the church would fall for very sound; and then, in a moment, with a cry, head up, arms high in the air, sweat pouring from his forehead, and all his body dancing as if it would never stop. Sometimes he did not stop until he fell—until he dropped like some animal felled by a hammer—moaning, on his face. And then, a great moaning filled the church.[12]

Gospel historian Tony Heilbut describes James Cleveland's praise and worship in a similar fashion:

> When moved by something, the spirit, a well-phrased line, *a high note by any of the male sopranos he likes to feature*, he'll rub his head and make a pained face, moaning "Ooooh." It's a spirited, orgasmic kind of pain, and if it continues, he'll bang his feet . . . . When he shouts, he tends to turn in position, take a few backward steps, then kick forth with Holy Ghost Abandon.[13]

In both instances the conjuring of the spirit through music manifests through a sexualized body. Baldwin's description of Elisha's piano playing sounds more like a description of sexual intercourse, especially since the reader knows that he is viewed through the longing eyes of the novel's protagonist John. And, Heilbut's description of Cleveland catching the spirit also implies Cleveland's queerness since his "shout" was brought on by "a high note by any of the male sopranos he likes to feature."

Beyond the manifestation of the spirit another vehicle for pushing the boundaries between secular and the sacred is the "costuming" for certain roles like the choir or preacher's robe.

The robe itself is a literal form of excess expressed when excessive material making up its sleeves and bodice bellows and balloons when caught up in wind. Thus, during spirit possession, directing the choir, or twirling down the aisle, the robe's expanded volume compliments the excess of the performance itself and also functions for "cross" purposes—a celebration of spirit and cross dressing. Freddie, a narrator in *Sweet Tea*, suggests the following about the choir robe: "This might sound really silly. That robe is very much like a dress. And they carry on and shout in that sort of legitimate dress . . . I have observed gay men really shouting and carrying on in these robes—working the robe."[14] Given these narratives, we come to recognize how the "props and costumes"—tambourines and robes—of the worship service are deployed for duplicitous purposes: they are integral to the conjuring of the spirit but also provide a space to perform non-normative gender and sexual identity.

The church, however, is not always a hospitable place for its LGBT members. Many struggle with reconciling their spirituality and sexuality because of the condemnation they receive from the pulpit and congregation, despite the integral role they play in the church. Ordained minister and cultural critic Michael Dyson captured this contradiction well: "A black minister will preach against sexual ills, especially homosexuality. At the close of the sermon, a soloist, who everybody knows is gay, will rise to perform a moving number, as the preacher extends an invitation to visitors to join the church. The soloist is, in effect, being asked to sing, and to sign, his theological death sentence."[15] Unfortunately, many queer church members choose to endure this bigotry because their church family is their first family—in other words, it was their community before they came to an understanding of their sexuality. Thus, leaving the church once one comes to term with his or her sexuality is not as easy as it may seem. In the worst-case scenario, many queer churchgoers begin to internalize the homophobia of the church and engage in the very bigotry and condemnation that they themselves fall victim to.

This is why so many popular gospel singers are closeted about their sexuality. They spit fire and brimstone in their concerts yet, behind closed doors indulge their homosexual desires. One of the more popular of these "ex-gay" singers is Donnie McClurkin. Born and raised in Copiague, New York, in 1959, McClurkin's childhood was filled with tragedies and traumas. Before the age of thirteen, he had experienced the death of his two-year-old brother who was hit and killed by a speeding car, and had been raped by an uncle and later by his uncle's son. McClurkin's aunt, who sang background vocals for gospel singer and composer Andre Crouch, rescued him from his family dysfunction. After staying close to Crouch throughout his boyhood, he began to play piano and sing with his church youth choir. He formed the McClurkin

Figure 5. E. Patrick Johnson. Courtesy of the author.

123

Singers by the time he was a teenager and later established the New York Restoration Choir. He now has his own church, Perfecting Faith Church in New York, which boasts more than one thousand members. McClurkin has spoken out against homosexuality on several occasions. He states that homosexuality is a spiritual issue, from which one can be delivered from by the power and grace of God. In his book *Eternal Victim/Eternal Victor*, he says that he came to the realization that his homosexuality was abnormal and not a part of God's plan.[16] He then described himself as having gone through a process by which he became "a saved and sanctified man." Despite twenty years of being gay, in one fell swoop, McClurkin disavowed his homosexuality and began preaching openly against it and accusing black men of the church as being sexual predators. While McClurkin's self-hatred is one extreme example, it does reflect how difficult it is for queer churchgoers to come to terms with their spirituality and sexuality in a way that leaves them feeling like whole individuals. How ironic then, that one of McClurkin's more popular songs, "Stand," is a testament to how one can overcome his or her internal struggles with spirituality and sexuality if they just holdfast to their conviction that they are fearfully and wonderfully made.

Many of these gifted voices, magical hands, and eloquent speakers have been taken away from us, but they have left an indelible mark on a music that comforts the soul and conjures the spirit. They have also laid the groundwork for queer musicians who have come after them, some of whom do not have to hide their sexuality, such as hip-hop gospel singer, Tonéx, who to date is the only male gospel singer to acknowledge his homosexuality.[17] In her article on the scandal in the gospel music industry brought on by Tonéx's coming out, Kelefe Sanneh writes:

> Gospel music has offered generations of same-gender-loving singers a place to call home, in exchange for their obedience, or their silence. This tricky and sometimes hard bargain shaped the genre, guiding its transfigured love songs, its expressions of praise and sorrow, its twinning of the orthodox and the outrageous. And there's no telling what gospel will sound like when that tacit arrangement no longer holds.[18]

As gospel music continues to morph, to speak to the daily struggles and challenges as well as to the tastes of its listeners, hopefully the queer brothers and sisters who are a part of the church family will be able to worship openly and proudly.

ENDNOTES
1. Quoted in Tony Heilbut, *The Gospel Sound: Good News in Bad Times* (New York: Simon and Schuster), 65.
2. Gayle Wald, *Shout, Sister, Shout!: The Untold Story of a Rock-and-Roll Trailblazer* (Boston: Beacon, 2007), 90.
3. Clarence Boyer, *How Sweet the Sound: The Golden Age of Gospel* (Washington, D.C.: Elliott and Clark, 1995), 159; my emphasis.
4. Wald, *Shout, Sister, Shout!,* 91.
5. Heilbut, *The Gospel Sound,* 233.
6. Willa Ward Royster, *How I Got Over: Clara Ward and the World-Famous Ward Singers* (Philadelphia: Temple University Press, 1997), 68–69.
7. John Howard, *Men Like That: A Southern Queer History* (Chicago: University of Chicago Press, 1999), 5.
8. Wald, *Shout, Sister, Shout!,* 87–88.
9. For more on Willmer's gender, see Tony Heilbut's liner notes to the compilation album *Kings of the Gospel Highway* (Shanatchie 2000).

10. For a great biography of Sylvester, see Joshua Gamson, *The Fabulous Sylvester: The Legend, the Music, the Seventies in San Francisco* (New York: Henry Holt, 2005).

11. E. Patrick Johnson, *Sweet Tea: Black Gay Men of the South—An Oral History* (Chapel Hill: University of North Carolina Press), 360–62.

12. James Baldwin, *Go Tell It on the Mountain* (New York: Dell, 1952), 15–16.

13. Heilbut, *The Gospel Sound*, 239; emphasis added.

14. Johnson, *Sweet Tea*, 217.

15. Michael Eric Dyson, *Race Rules: Navigating the Color Line* (Reading: Addison-Wesley, 1996), 105.

16. Donnie McClurkin, *Eternal Victim / Eternal Victor* (Lanham: Pneuma Life, 2001).

17. For more on Tonéx's coming-out story, see Kelefa Sanneh, "Revelations," *The New Yorker*, February 8, 2010.

18. Sanneh, "Revelations": 56.

Toward an Archive of Latina/o Queer Chicago
Art, Politics, and Social Performance

Lawrence La Fountain-Stokes, Lourdes Torres, and Ramón H. Rivera-Servera

The archives, written histories, and media representations of gay and lesbian activism and culture in the United States have not generally acknowledged a Latina/o presence. When accounts have focused specifically on queer Latinas/os, they have rarely landed in Chicago, offering us instead a bicoastal map that almost exclusively focuses on that well-rehearsed triumvirate of Latina/o queer mythology: New York, Los Angeles, and San Francisco.[1] This essay is in large part an invitation to engage with the history of queer Latinas/os in Chicago by promoting further documentation and circulation of knowledge about this significant and vital component of the queer community. The diversity of sites, practices, and communities introduced here highlight the historically strong and presently thriving Latino queer community in this city. This essay offers but an introduction to the plethora of historical materials to be found in the many personal archives, political and artistic ephemera, and individual and collective memories that evidence a Latina/o queer presence in Chicago.

I. *Entrando por La Cueva:* On the Geographies of Latina/o Queer Chicago

Chicago has had a strong Latina/o presence since the beginning of the twentieth century, when large numbers of Mexicans arrived escaping the unsettling conditions of the Mexican Revolution and attracted by the growth in industrial and agricultural labor opportunities in the Midwest with a steady flow continuing to the present when over 1.3 million Mexicans reside in the Chicago metropolitan region.[2] They were followed by a sizeable migration of Puerto Ricans, who arrived during the 1940s to assume positions in the thriving steel industry and as domestic laborers. They currently form the second largest group of Latinas/os in Chicago, numbering over 150,000. Cubans, which constitute the fourth-largest group at close to 19,000, began to arrive in large groups during the 1950s, with a second wave arriving in the city from 1960 to 1973 as exiles of the Fidel Castro government; a third wave relocated from the Mariel boatlift in the 1980s, while a fourth wave of *balseros* came to the region in the 1990s. Guatemalans (presently the third-largest Latina/o group in the city at an estimated 30,000) and Salvadorans (8,000) migrated in large numbers during the 1980s as part of the Sanctuary Movement, which offered refuge to residents of war-torn Central American nations. The city of Chicago is home to communities of Latinas/os from every single Latin American national origin with Ecuadorans, Colombians, and Peruvians numbering with populations of over 10,000.

In 2010, the Latina/o population approached the two-million mark in the metropolitan region and will soon constitute a third of the total population in the city of Chicago.[3] It is diverse in national, ethnic, racial, and class makeup; including affluent and professional Latin Americans, political refugees, and economic migrants alike. Overwhelmingly a working-class community with a sizeable and growing middle class, Latina/o Chicago boasts what is arguably one of the most diverse Latina/o demographic profiles in the nation.

With over a century old presence in Chicago, Latina/os of varying ethnic and national backgrounds have a shared history of social, economic, and cultural proximity. Relations across groups of origin characterize the experience of many residents of Latin American descent who establish social and cultural networks in Chicago that exceed traditional narratives of national belonging. They create new intersections, both identitarian and affective, that result in an increasingly inter-Latina/o city. These intersections are palpable in the queer social networks that developed throughout the city, most prominently since the 1980s, when Latina/o queer-specific cultural, political, and social efforts began to appear in most affirmative and public ways.

The now famous Latina/o drag club La Cueva located in the Mexican enclave of La Villita is one prominent example of both the history and often-tacit presence

Ketty Teanga. From *Colorlines Magazine* (July-August 2006). Photograph by Robert Thornton.

of Latina/o queer life in the city of Chicago.[4] La Cueva is located in the southwest corridor of the city, a combination of nineteenth-century industrial and residential development initially occupied by Bohemian and Irish immigrants and now constituting the largest Mexican neighborhood in Chicago. The club began as a single event hosted by Ketty Teanga—an Ecuadoran-born drag queen who since age eleven lived with her mother and Puerto Rican stepfather in New York and Puerto Rico—at another La Villita historic gay watering hole, El Infierno. Due to its popularity, it soon moved to the owner's larger establishment, La Cueva.[5] Credited as being one of the oldest Latina/o drag clubs in the country still in operation, La Cueva does not boast a flashy identifying street sign nor the roped-off entrances of Chicago's Boystown establishments.[6] Instead the plain white wood-paneled and quasi-anonymous façade of the single-story building insinuates itself subtly within the Mexican business district that surrounds it. Here, within the second largest business district in the city, working-class gay Latinos, and increasingly Latinas, have drunk, danced together, and witnessed for close to three decades the spectacular performances of Latina drag queens impersonating the vast repertoires of Latin American and U.S. Latina/o popular music from *bolero* and *ranchera* divas to *salsa* queens and the more recent bubble-gum Mexican pop stars.[7]

Despite the long histories of queer Latina/o presence in the city and the existence of pioneer spaces and performers such as those found in La Cueva, our history remains for the most part unknown. Hidden behind the unassuming façades of marginal geographies often rendered mute by the LGBT mainstream, the history Latina/o queer Chicago often recedes into the realm of invisibility. La Cueva is but one such site, historical event, and community in need of recognition, documentation, and celebration as part of queer history, Latina/o history, and Chicago history. Another example is how Latina lesbian organizers in Chicago helped to develop social and political communities. Latino queer artists have similarly created spaces where Latino and queer interests, passions, and desires meet, clash, and dance along with the messiness of inhabiting the intersections between queer, ethnic, and racial experiences. Latina/o queer Chicago is a palpable if little-acknowledged presence in the queer geographies of the region.

In the pages that follow we introduce important organizations like Latina Lesbians en Nuestro Ambiente (LLENA) and Amigas Latinas and artists such as Achy Obejas, Rane Arroyo, Rose Troche, Coya Paz, and Fausto Fernós. As a reader we hope you become familiar with these names but also with the important work—social, political, artistic—that each of these groups or individuals have done and continue to do to make Latino queer life in Chicago the pleasurable, at times a little painful, but always richly textured experience it has been, continues to be, and certainly will be for a long time to come. This is not an exhaustive survey of the history of social, political, and artistic efforts by and on behalf of Latina/o queer Chicago. Instead, this essay offers a glimpse into the archives and focus areas of each of us as scholars invested in documenting aspects of this history.

II. Latina Lesbian Organizing in Chicago

In the late 1980s, there were not many spaces in Chicago that openly welcomed Latina lesbians. This changed when Maria Amparo Jiménez, a Mexican who had just moved to Chicago from Mexico City, called for a meeting of Latina lesbians in *Outlines* (a Chicago-based gay newspaper). Ten women showed up to their first meeting in November 1988; subsequent meetings in those early days often drew between thirty to forty women. The group decided to call itself LLENA, an acronym for Latina Lesbians en Nuestro Ambiente (in our space). Marilyn Morales came up with the name after a few meetings of the group, "LLENA was perfect because that's how it was at the beginning, we were in our

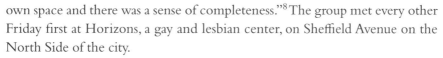

LLENA (Latina Lesbians en Nuestro Ambiente). Mona Noriega Collection.

own space and there was a sense of completeness."[8] The group met every other Friday first at Horizons, a gay and lesbian center, on Sheffield Avenue on the North Side of the city.

A few years later, some members of the group expressed a desire to meet in one of their Latino neighborhoods so that the meeting would be more accessible to Latinas. LLENA members also felt unwelcome at Horizons, which they experienced as a mostly gay male space. LLENA leaders eventually accepted the invitation of José Lopez, the executive director of the Puerto Rican Cultural Center, to meet at its space in Humboldt Park, in the heart of the Puerto Rican community. This was an example of an early push to establish a public lesbian presence within a predominantly heterosexual Latino space. Initially, some of LLENA's members were reluctant to meet at the Puerto Rican Cultural Center because of its reputation for radical activism around the independence of Puerto Rico during the late 1980s and early 1990s. Even though the center was a frequent target of FBI surveillance and harassment, the group opted to meet there.[9]

As LLENA members recall, the meetings drew all kinds of Latinas. While the original organizers were mostly first-generation, Spanish-speaking immigrants, they welcomed all Latinas no matter how they identified. According to former members, the meetings were intense, bilingual, and chaotic.[10] They often lasted more than four hours. The meetings drew scores of women of all Latin American national backgrounds (Puerto Rican, Mexican, Cuban, Ecuadoran, and Colombian). They attracted women of all ages (from their early twenties to sixty-year-olds), married or closeted women, women who were just coming out, veteran dykes, professional women, undocumented women, and women from all class backgrounds. LLENA provided a space for all these women who never before had a place of their own.[11] From the beginning, members of LLENA were also keenly interested in organizing not just Latina lesbians, but lesbians of all races and ethnicities. They had an expansive vision of who they were and they were clearly committed from the beginning to building bridges between Chicago Latina lesbians and other women, both women of color and white women locally, nationally, and internationally.

LLENA's orientation toward coalitional building and its trans-national vision were very much in line with the feminist politics and organizing being articulated across the U.S. at the time. In the late 1980s, there was much excitement about the possibility of creating a Third World Women of Color feminist movement. Feminist women of color offered a stinging critique of white mainstream feminism at the same time that they began to promote the building of a third world women's movement that would offer a more nuanced analysis of multiple identities, the simultaneity of oppression, and the urgent need for coalitional politics and organizing.[12]

Another of LLENA's more successful projects involved living up to its mission by organizing with lesbians of all colors. LLENA cosponsored the International Women's Dance in the late 1980s and early 1990s that brought together thousands of women in annual dances. The first dances were held in 1989 at the Electricians Union Hall on South Ashland. As the dances grew, they moved downtown to the Congress Hotel on Michigan Avenue. There they attracted more than fifteen hundred women to the event. This effort led to the building of working relationships, networking, and friendships among women of many different backgrounds who organized the dance. Among the other organizations that cosponsored the events were progressive groups of working-class women of color such as the Chicago Women in Trades, Literary Exchange, The Mozambican Women's Support Project, and Women United for a Better Chicago. Only organizations with a membership of at least 75-percent women of color were invited to cosponsor the event.[13]

LLENA members were very intentional about why they were committing to the International Women's Day Dances: they didn't see them solely as fundraising ventures, although this was an important element that motivated the work. According to the November 1991 minutes, the goals for the dance were: "1) to network/connect with other women's organizations, 2) to publicize each organization, 3) to work together acknowledging and respecting our differences, 4) to do something fun/social, 5) to celebrate international women's day, and 6) to work cooperatively sharing the benefits and work." While there was some debate as to whether to advertise the event as a lesbian or a women's dance, the organizers decided that they would attract more participation if they promoted the dance as simply a women's dance. A heated discussion surfaced every year about whether or not to allow men to attend the dances. Some of the women felt strongly that all their events should be exclusively women's spaces, while others felt comfortable with supportive male family, friends, and allies. In fact, the degree to which the group should work and form coalitions with men led to fiercely contentious debates. In terms of the International Women's Day Dance, the group decided that they would welcome the financial support of men but they made it clear that they preferred that men not attend the dances. The policy that prevailed was that "men would be allowed but not encouraged."[14]

133

LLENA was especially interested in building coalitions with women of color but they also worked with white women. The fall 1990 issue of their bilingual newsletter *Lesbiana* highlights LLENA's expansive vision of who they were as an organization and makes clear their commitment to enacting an inclusive and pluralistic Latina lesbian feminism.[15] One article states, "In as much as this newsletter will contribute to our visibility and further enrich the lesbian community in Chicago, we also hope that it will help build bridges between our community and the Asian, African American, and white/Anglo lesbian communities." The April 1990 minutes recorded a presentation to the group by Sarah Hoagland, a noted white feminist philosopher who was then-leader of a group called CLEAR (Chicago Lesbians Emerging Against Racism). CLEAR was a white, feminist, lesbian separatist group that offered to fundraise to send some of the Latinas to the Fifth Feminist Gathering (Encuentro) of Latin American Lesbian Women held in Costa Rica in 1990. LLENA members recall that there were various responses to these political presentations. Some women actively engaged with the ideas presented, while others listened politely but were more interested in socializing with their Latina lesbian sisters rather than listening to white lesbians discussing feminist separatist politics.[16]

LESBIANA
LESBIANAS LATINAS EN NUESTRO AMBIENTE (L.L.E.N.A.)

FALL 1990	VOL. 1	No.1

¡ESTAMOS AQUI PARA QUEDARNOS!

Van a ser casi dos años, el próximo 4 de noviembre, desde que, en 1988, un grupo de ocho lesbianas latinas, nos reuníamos por primera vez. Trafamos la idea de crear y mantener un espacio en donde toda latina lesbiana de Chicago y los suburbios pudiera encontrar el apoyo, la confiencialidad, el aliento y el afecto necesarios para aceptar y fortalecer nuestra propia identidad.

Queríamos también redescubrir y alentar el desarrollo del potencial de liderazgo de nuestras compañeras, de tal manera que en el futuro pudiéramos tener una auténtica y efectiva representatividad en la comunidad de mujeres, la latina, y la homosexual de Chicago -- y por que no, también a nivel nacional e internacional.

Queríamos también lograr todo lo antes dicho, en el contexto de nuestra etnicidad y herencia cultural, como la base para luchar contra el racismo, el sexismo, el clasismo, individualismo y la homofobia que permea la sociedad en la que vivimos todos.

Estos últimos dos años han sido difíciles, ¡y hermosos! Al mismo tiempo que hemos crecido, hemos aprendido que queda mucho por hacer. Comprendemos que para poder realizar nuestros objetivos como grupo, debemos trabajar entre nosotras nuestras diferencias: de origen, formas de vida, perspectivas de vida, posiciones políticas, y nuestra propia homofobia. Este es el reto que se nos presenta de inmediato y lo aceptamos.

LLENA es una semilla que ha empezado a germinar, está creciendo. Ahora es una plantita relativamente nueva, está fresca y demanda nuestra dedicación y amor constantes. Esta plantita se hará un árbol grande, fuerte, frondoso, con ramas que reflejen nuestros diferentes colores, aromas y formas. Las raíces de este árbol son comunes a todas, son nuestra fuerza. La savia que corre por las venas de este árbol del presente y el futuro, nos alimenta y nos hará más fuertes y seguras cada día. Mientras vamos haciendo el camino queremos invitarte compañera latina lesbiana a que con tu activa presencia, con tus ideas, y tu trabajo solidario, nos ayudes a lograr nuestros objetivos. ¡Estamos aquí para quedarnos! Llámanos o escríbenos apenas termines de leer esta primera boletina. Nuestras reuniones son bilingües, español / inglés.

Un abrazo,
C. Aguilar

WE ARE HERE TO STAY!

November fourth, 1990, will mark two years since a group of Latina lesbians, myself included, first met with the intention of creating and maintaining a space in which every Latina lesbian in Chicago and surrounding areas would find the support, confidentiality, encouragement and affection necessary to come to terms with her identity.

We also wanted to start encouraging the development of potential leadership abilities in our compañeras, so as to begin building a strong and influential Latina lesbian presence in the Latino, women's, and gay and lesbian communities of Chicago. And why stop there; this presence, we thought, could potentially expand nationally as well as internationally.

Above all, we wanted to achieve all of the aforementioned within the context of our ethnic and cultural backgrounds, as a means by which to combat the racism, sexism, individualism, and homophobia which permeate the society in which we all live.

The past two years have been difficult. But, we have grown, and we have become more aware of the tasks that lie before us. We have come to understand that in order to fulfill our objectives, we have to first work at achieving the understanding and respect necessary for dealing with the barriers created by dynamics such as differences in backgrounds, lifestyles, political, and philosophical perspectives, etc. This is our challenge.

Right now LLENA is a seed, barely germinating -- it is a young and vulnerable plant that needs our love and dedication. It will become a strong and beautiful tree whose branches will have the different colors, aromas and shapes which characterize us as individuals. But we must remember that the roots of that tree are the same for all of us and that they are our strength; they provide the sap that will feed us and make us stronger day by day. With that strength we shall be able to provide a supportive and safe environment for other compañeras.

In the meantime, LLENA is here to stay! and we want to encourage the participation of more Latina lesbians (we know you exist) in our group. Our meetings are bilingual: Spanish and English. Call or write to us as soon as you are done reading this newsletter!

Un abrazo,
C. Aguilar

Lesbiana Newsletter of LLENA.

134

In its short life, LLENA promoted its expansive vision, organized successful political, social, and cultural events, and had a strong record of successful networking across communities. In 1993, only five years since their first organizational meeting, LLENA disbanded. Former members suggest that class, political, and language issues ultimately divided the group and led to its disintegration. Others say that differences of opinion about the direction of the group lead to the formation of factions and the ensuing infighting. Still others suggest that personal relationships and dating within the organization lead to conflicts and hurt feelings that destroyed the group.[17]

Members who participated in LLENA believe that lessons learned from the earlier attempt at Latina lesbian organizing in Chicago may have prevented similar issues from disrupting Amigas Latinas, the Latina lesbian organization that followed it.[18] As Tracy Baim documents in *Out and Proud in Chicago*, Chicago in the mid-1990s experienced a proliferation of organizing by queer people of color.[19] Ethnic identity groups such as Affinity and Chicago Black Lesbians (two groups that represented African American lesbians), Khuli Zaban, (a group that represented South Asian and West Asian queer women), and ALMA (the Association of Latino Men for Action) formed. Amigas Latinas,

En La Vida Newsletter.

like many of these other organizations, was actually a splinter group that developed from a larger, multiethnic group, Women of all Colors and Cultures Together (WACT) that hosted potluck lunches once a month throughout the 1990s. One of the founders of WACT, Evette Cardona, was also a founder of Amigas Latinas.

In the summer of 1995, several years after the demise of LLENA, Evette Cardona and a small group of Latina lesbians decided it was again time to bring together Latina lesbians. One source of inspiration was ALMA (The Association of Latino Men for Action), a group that began organizing Latino gay men in the mid 1990s.[20] Initially conceived of as a support group for lesbians and bisexuals, Amigas Latinas has established itself as a strong and visible organization that advocates for the Latina lesbian, bisexual, transgender, and questioning (LBTQ) community in Chicago. Amigas Latinas is unique because it is one of the few Latina lesbian organizations in the United States that has sustained itself over a decade and continues to meet the needs of the Latina lesbian community. In 2003, Amigas Latinas achieved not-for-profit organizational status and has grown to over three hundred members. Through its various programs, Amigas Latinas works to educate and empower queer Latinas, as well as to educate service providers, the Latino community, the general gay community and legislators about the issues relevant to the Latina LBTQ community.

An important difference between LLENA and Amigas Latinas was the political context out of which each of the groups emerged. Chicago in the late 1990s and 2000s was a much friendlier place for Latino gays and lesbians than during the 1980s. Remarking on this change and LLENA's contribution, Morales (a member of both LLENA and Amigas Latinas) notes, "We put Latina women on the map in terms of what was going on in the 80s as far as the gay scene, I mean there's Boystown, you had all these gay groups, it's all white affiliated.... It was not easy being gay, in the '80s. The gay scene was like, no one talked about it in the Latino community; it was horrible.... So I think that LLENA really kind of cemented that there is this population in the Latino community that is gay, and we are here."[21]

Several factors can explain Amigas' sustainability. Amigas Latinas has survived as long as it has because it recognizes that Latinas are not a monolithic group. Amigas attempts to make a place for Latinas of different nationalities, language preferences, age groups, and sexual identifications. It provides regular ongoing programming to Latina LGBTQ with diverse interests. It offers programs for youth, older women, and families, as well as social and educational events that attempt to bring all these interests together. Amigas also regularly surveys its membership about the direction Amigas should take. Invariably, women declare that the space created by Amigas is crucial to their lives: "During my coming out process, the camaraderie of Amigas Latinas really assisted me in this process. Amigas has always been like a family for me, they will always be there for women who need a place to be herself without fear or retribution. The comfort of being with people like yourself is an incredible strength and gives tremendous support! I am completely grateful that Amigas Latinas exists and provides a safe place for women who love women. Thank you."[22] Similar responses consistently appear throughout the fifteen years of Amigas Latinas' existence.

This is not to suggest that attempts to navigate differences don't sometimes challenge the group cohesion. For example, several years ago, some members of the board lobbied to modify the mission of the organization so as to include transgender Latinas. At that time Amigas' mission specified that the organization advocated for lesbian and bisexual rights. Not everyone agreed, but the majority of the board voted to change the mission to also represent and advocate for transgendered Latinas, and to run a series of programs educating the

Amigas Latinas Float in Chicago Gay Pride Parade. Evette Cardona Collection.

membership about the issues of Latinas who identified as transgender. This was a top-down decision that was not meet with universal approval by the board and the membership, but most of the group's board members felt that this was the right thing to do.

Both LLENA and Amigas Latinas expanded the options for Latina lesbians in Chicago. They offered (and Amigas Latinas continues to offer) a space for queer Latinas to meet other queer Latinas and to discuss issues that were central to our lives. LLENA was the first organization to offer Latina lesbians a space (outside of the few bars where Latina lesbians felt welcome) to call their own. With its diverse membership that included immigrant, Spanish monolingual first-generation Latinas, second-generation, English-dominant women, married, older closeted women, twenty-year-old new dykes, etc., LLENA worked to bring this complex community together with its vision of a transnational, global lesbian feminism. Unfortunately, LLENA was not successful at mediating all the differences within the group and at dealing with internal group dynamics but it offered an inspiring early example of Latina lesbian organizing. Amigas has been successful at sustaining its organization through a strategy of offering a wide range of programs for the diverse constituents of the Chicago Latina

El Poder de Ser Transgenero y Latino!

Te gustaria aprender mas sobre la dinamica y el poder de la identificacion y construccion de ser transgenero y Latino?

Amigas Latinas Grupo Juventud te invita a un presentacion y taller con Sebastián Colón, un transgénero Boricua radical, poeta, artista y luchador por los derechos humanos. Hijo de madre soltera y católica. Sebastián es hoy día estudinante graduado en la Universidad de Michigan. El nació y crecio en Puerto Rico, donde trabajó como activista lesbiana radical y organizador comunitario por alrededor de 10 años. Despues de salir del closet como transgénero en el 1999, Sebastián se mudó a Austin, Texas donde continuó su trabajo como activista y su lucha por la justicia social. Sebastián se identifica como FTS – *"female to something else!"*

Do you want to learn more about the dynamics and power of Latino transgender identity?

Amigas Latinas Youth Group invites you to a presentation and workshop with Sebastián Colón, a radical Boricua transgender activist, poet, performer and social warrior. He is the son/daughter of a single catholic mother and a graduate student at the University of Michigan. Sebastián grew up in Puerto Rico, where he was out as a radical lesbian and community organizer for more than 10 years. After coming out as a transgender person in 1998, he moved to Austin, Texas where he continued his work as an activist and his constant fight for social justice. He identifies as FTS -- female to something else!

Ven a escuchar, aprender y comparte tus historias y experencias con otras jovenes LBTQ. Come learn, listen and share your stories & experiences with other LBTQ youth!

Center on Halsted | 2855 N. Lincoln | Octubre/October 6, 2006 | 6:00pm – 8:00pm
Para mas informacion/For more info llame/call
312-409-5697 or info@amigaslatinas.org

138

Flyer for a 2006 Amigas Latinas event at the Center on Halsted.

queer community while it has also worked to bridge national and international issues through its work around immigrant rights. It continues to meet the challenges posed by differing agendas and shifting identifications.

In addition to Amigas Latinas and ALMA, several new queer Latino groups have recently organized in Chicago, including Orgullo en Acción and Boricua Pride. Young Latinos have been at the center of much new queer organizing. In the last few years Chicago youth have held an annual Latino Queer Prom. Since 2002, Radio Arte (a youth-run public radio station, funded primarily by the National Museum of Mexican Art) has produced Homofrecuencia, the first Spanish-language radio program in U.S. history that targets LGBTQ youth and allies. Pedro Serrano recently founded Readers of Queer Latino Literature, a group of mostly young Latino males who get together one a month to discuss queer books and readings. Two other more recent Chicago Latina cultural organizations, La Dulce Palabra Spoken Word Ensemble (which has been documented by the filmmaker Linda García Merchant) and Teatro Luna, showcase queer Latina experience.[23]

III. Queer Latina/o Arts and Culture in Chicago

The work of cultural and political organizations such as LLENA, Amigas Latinas, and ALMA and the social relations developed at places such as La Cueva and Circuito (the Latin Night held at Circuit Night Club in Boystown) is complemented by the artistic productions of Chicago-based queer Latina and Latino cartoonists, filmmakers, performers, podcasters and writers who have focused their attention on the rich and enormously varied queer experience of this city. One key example is the openly gay radical political cartoonist Daniel (Danny) Sotomayor (1958-92), who was born in Humboldt Park and was of Mexican and Puerto Rican descent; his fearless editorial cartoons and activist work denouncing the AIDS crisis were a fundamental contribution to American society.[24] Authors such as the lesbian Cuban-American novelist, short-story writer, journalist, and poet Achy Obejas and the gay Puerto Rican poet, short-story author, and playwright Rane Arroyo have portrayed the realities of characters caught between Chicago and the Caribbean, who negotiate linguistic, cultural, and social differences along with their divergent sexual orientation. Filmmakers such as Tadeo García (who directed *On the Downlow* in 2004) have portrayed relationships between young Latino men who do not publicly identify as gay, and the challenges they face in negotiating their sexualities and desires. In her widely distributed and very memorable debut film *Go Fish* (1994), the lesbian Puerto Rican director Rose Troche conjured an utopian vision of young, multiracial lesbian integration in Wicker Park in the early 1990s. More recently, the lesbian Peruvian American Coya Paz and the pan-Latina ensemble Teatro Luna have showcased the experience of diverse Latina women in Chicago (for example, in their extraordinary multi-voiced, collectively written play *S-E-X-Oh!*), while the gay Puerto Rican podcaster and performance artist Fausto Fernós has been putting Chicago on the international map in his multiple-award-winning *Feast of Fun* show, produced five days a week from his home in Andersonville, in which he, Marc Felion, and many collaborators and guests prominently discuss queer Latina/o experience in the Windy City. In this section, we will briefly showcase the work of some of these artists and see what they tell us about queer and LGBT Latina/o life in Chicago. These are just a few examples of a much larger group.

139

Achy Obejas

The Cuban-American writer Achy Obejas was born in Cuba in 1956 and came to the United States with her family in 1962. She is the author of a book of short stories titled *We Came All the Way from Cuba So You Could Dress Like This?*

AIDS activist Danny Sotomayor stormed the Chicago International Film Festival, October 24, 1988, to protest Illinois Governor James R. Thompson's approval of HIV antibody tests without patient consent. Photo by Rex Wockner/*Chicago Outlines* newspaper.

Fausto Fernós and Marc Felion, Feast of Fun podcast. Design by Fausto Fernós (2009).

Achy Obejas
(2010). Courtesy of
Achy Obejas.

(1994) and several novels including *Memory Mambo* (1996) and *Days of Awe* (2001).[25] All of these books are marked by the author's interest in exploring the experiences of queer Latinas in Chicago.

The stories included in *We Came All the Way from Cuba so You Could Dress Like This?* introduce us to a Latina/o Chicago cultural geography of neighborhoods, families, accidents, relationships, tears, laughter, and joy. This exploration of space, geography and identity continues in *Memory Mambo*, a novel that tells the story of Juani, a twenty-four-year-old Cuban-American lesbian in Logan Square who hasn't gone to college and works in her family's laundromat.

Memory Mambo centers around the protagonist's desire for knowledge about Cuba and for an identity as a young person in the Midwestern United States. Juani does not seem inclined to celebrate the duplicity of her cultural/national experience, but rather seems stuck in a cultural and existential void of not really knowing who she is or what she wants, lacking control over the direction in which her life is going.

Obejas's novel is framed by Juani's breakup with her Puerto Rican closeted lesbian girlfriend, Gina, who is a radical *independentista* (or pro-independence advocate) and works on the political campaign of a Puerto Rican alderman candidate. The frailty of Cuban national-ethnic identification in a strongly multi-cultural environment in the United States (that is to say, outside of Miami's Little Havana) is highlighted in this novel through inter-ethnic relations, in the context of the prejudiced views that each group has about each other. Cubans and Puerto Ricans are shown stereotyping each other mercilessly, making fun of the particular historical circumstances that have determined so

141

much of these groups' experience in the United States. The conservative political views of exiled Cubans regarding the Revolution are pitted against nationalist Puerto Ricans' desire for a free, independent homeland. The relative economic superiority of Cuban exiles, often times fostered by disproportionate U.S. government assistance, is compared to the chronic poverty of the Puerto Ricans, who are portrayed in a negative light.

The fact that this novel is set in Chicago is meaningful given the very particular dynamics of inter-Latina/o relationships in the city. Scholars such as Félix Padilla, Ana Yolanda Ramos-Zayas, and Nicholas de Genova have extensively analyzed Puerto Rican and Mexican interactions in Chicago, also discussing (to a much more limited extent) the Cuban presence.[26] In her book *National Performances*, Ramos-Zayas discusses Cuban/Puerto Rican tensions originating from disagreements over leftist, nationalist-oriented politics: she analyzes how Daniel Alvarez, a Latino officer of the Chicago Park District and the son of a Cuban father and a Puerto Rican mother was portrayed as "un cubano" due to his opposition to erecting a statue of the Puerto Rican Nationalist leader Pedro Albizu Campos. This tension taps into deep-seated perceptions (correct or incorrect) of Cubans as anti-communist conservatives and Puerto Ricans as anticolonial radicals. Yet, according to scholar Erika Gisela Abad, the inherent heterosexism and patriarchal structure of dominant Puerto Rican cultural and political organizations in the city also provokes problems for women and for queer Puerto Ricans.[27]

Questions of Latina bisexuality acquire a more nuanced representation in Obejas's 2001 novel *Days of Awe*. Here, the Cuban American protagonist Alejandra San José is portrayed as a bisexual woman raised in Chicago who discovers her family's Jewish identity and decides to travel back to Cuba to learn about her family but also herself, sexually, religiously, and otherwise. *Days of Awe* signals a more mature, sophisticated stage of Obejas's writing, in which she is able to account for very complex interethnic, multireligious, and transnational phenomena. The portrayal of Latinos in Chicago is also more expansive that in most dominant representations.

Rane Arroyo

Born in Chicago to Puerto Rican migrant parents, Rane Ramón Arroyo (1954-2010) was a prize-winning poet and playwright who also lived in Ohio and Pennsylvania, where he received a Ph.D. in American Literature and Cultural Studies at the University of Pittsburgh. A self-professed gay writer, he

Rane Arroyo (2003). Courtesy of Glenn Sheldon.

was also a literary critic and performance artist, and taught in the University of Toledo's Creative Writing program for many years. Arroyo's work is marked by his references to Caribbean and Latino life in the Midwest (particularly in Chicago), by his consistent engagement with canonical literary figures of American and English modernism as well as with Latin American and Spanish poets, and by his exploration of his own personal experiences, including his longstanding relationship with the poet Glenn Sheldon, his affection for his cat Diva, and his awareness of his own process of aging. He published ten books of poetry, including *The Singing Shark* (1996), *Pale Ramón* (1998), *Home Movies of Narcissus* (2002), and *Same-Sex Séances* (2008), plus a collection of short stories called *How To Name A Hurricane* (2005).[28]

Arroyo's self-reflexive poetry and fiction often focus on the inner conscience of a poetic persona, a gay Puerto Rican writer who feels out of place in the world and who is constantly struggling to grapple with what it means to be marked by racial, sexual, and linguistic difference. In this universe, poetry and fiction are construed as the space where memory comes together, the space for the appreciation of that which surrounds the individual, a way to come to terms with the world and to reflect about politics, news, racial relations, immigrant experience, and quite markedly, with what it means to be an American.

At the core of Arroyo's universe is his family and the Puerto Rican traditions (dance, music, food, the Spanish language) and social experiences (factory work, poverty, migration) that characterize them. There is a recurrent set of characters that reappear throughout many of Arroyo's books; these include Mami, Papi, Aunt Sylvia, Uncle "Rachel" (the transvestite uncle), as well as his many cousins. His poetry often expresses intimate (and evolving) relationships with these individuals, highlighting issues of masculinity and gender in relation to the father and uncle, of tradition and assimilation in relation to his mother, and of youth and coming of age with the cousins.

Arroyo's writing is marked by the variety of topics it covers in a most colloquial way, wandering from considerations of Latino popular and mass culture (Andy García, Antonio Banderas, Ricky Ricardo, Rita Moreno, *West Side Story*, Speedy González, and Taco Bell), to revisionist historic dialogues with Christopher Columbus and conquistadors such as Juan Ponce de León, to profound analysis about the specific environs of a particular neighborhood or serious critiques of racism or of the effects of drug trafficking and drug addiction. It is a poetry and fiction that tries to reconcile geographic specificity (his own love of Chicago and his parents' Puerto Rico) with cosmopolitanism (a learned engagement with the Western tradition and extensive travels throughout the world). There is a clear attempt to address dominant conceptions of Latinos in the United States, engaging with damaging stereotypes as well as with issues specific to Mexican-Americans/Chicanos, Cuban-Americans, and Puerto Ricans.

Arroyo's short story "X, My Ex" (in *How to Name a Hurricane*) is a good example of how the author tackles these topics.[29] "X, My Ex" focuses on the reminiscences of a first-person narrator, a Puerto Rican gay man named Emir who lives in Boystown, the main gay neighborhood in Chicago, and who tells of his relationship with a man dressed in a Zorro outfit (the "X" of the title) whom he meets "at one of those rooftop barbecues Chicago is famous for, where tenants bring out their potted plants and create green walls between the party and the city" (100). After a year of dating, Emir is dumped by "X," the white, previously heterosexual man from Utah whose name is never revealed. Chicago is marked by men such as "Jerry, a nice man known for cruising the johns at Wrigley Field whenever the Cubs were losing, or in other words, often" (101), by Emir's friend Linc, who calls him up to report a sighting of X "by the Belmont Rocks" (105), and by John, a friend with AIDS from Milwaukee who hangs himself. In this tender, vulnerable story, Chicago is a city populated by numerous gay men who have all slept with each other, where heartbreak is negotiated through alcohol, romantic reminiscences about Puerto Rico, and resistance to ex-boyfriend's special requests.

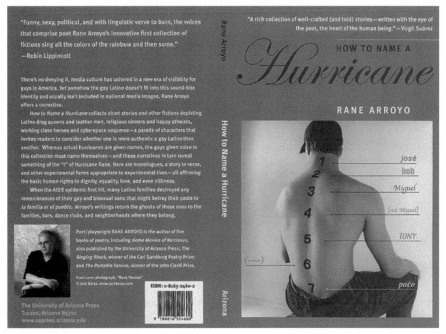

Cover of *How to Name a Hurricane* by Rane Arroyo.

Rose Troche

Rose Troche is a Chicago-born Puerto Rican filmmaker who has achieved significant mainstream commercial success, having her first feature-length narrative film *Go Fish* picked up for distribution by the Samuel Goldwyn Company at the Sundance Film Festival in 1994, then directing a high-budget English gay comedy (*Bedrooms and Hallways*, 1998), a major Hollywood film (*The Safety of Objects*, 2001, starring Glenn Close and Patricia Clarkson), and some of the most talked-about cable television programs in the U.S., including numerous episodes of Showtime's *The L Word* (a lesbian-focused series that she also cowrites, although one marked by its poor representation of Latinas) and one episode of HBO's *Six Feet Under.*

Her feature-length directorial debut *Go Fish* was cowritten and co-produced by Troche and her then-girlfriend Guinevere Turner; the film was initially conceptualized in August of 1991 and made in Chicago with an extremely limited budget and with nonprofessional volunteer actors.[30] *Go Fish* was a box-office success in 1994, achieving major national and international

From left to right: Migdalia Meléndez, Guinevere Turner, and T. Wendy McMillan in a video still from *Go Fish* (Rose Troche, 1994).

distribution, and has been frequently identified as a key component of the 1990s American "New Queer Cinema." It is often compared to Spike Lee's debut film *She's Gotta Have It* (1986) and described as doing for lesbian film what Lee did for African American cinema, a comparison that unfortunately is often read as devoid of racial/ethnic specificity and that by extension suggests it refers to "white" lesbian film. In spite (or perhaps because) of this, the film is very rarely considered to be a "Puerto Rican movie." Rather, people tend to see it as centered on the romantic experiences of two non-Latina white women—a young, trendy, somewhat angst-ridden writer/college student called Max (played by Guinevere Turner herself) and a dowdy, hippy-ish, slightly older veterinarian's assistant called Ely (V. S. Brodie)—in the context of a group of multiracial and multiethnic lesbian friends—a butch African American college teacher named Kia (T. Wendy McMillan); her girlfriend, a femme, semi-closeted, divorced Puerto Rican nurse named Evy (Migdalia Meléndez); and a sex-radical, "happily promiscuous," lesbian-identified, slightly butch young white bartender named Daria (Anastasia Sharp)—who conspire to bring Max and Ely together in early 1990s Chicago, specifically in Wicker Park, a neighborhood that before gentrification was a part of West

Town and that for a brief moment in the late 1980s and early 1990s had an important multicultural lesbian community.

Audiences' and (most) critics' lack of awareness about the Puerto Rican specificity of *Go Fish* has to do with widespread lack of knowledge about the history of Puerto Ricans in Chicago and also (and especially) with the subtle, almost incidental, and oblique treatment of this issue in the film: Wicker Park is not portrayed as a neighborhood with a Latino population (which it was, or had historically been, as Gina Pérez and Félix Padilla have noted), but rather as an artsy, bohemian, and lesbian one (i.e., the one it was becoming as a result of white artist and gay and lesbian migration and yuppy gentrification that started in the 1970s); the words "Puerto Rico" or "Puerto Rican" are never mentioned in the film; and while Evy and her mother speak Spanish and code-switch between Spanish and English, the only way to know that they are Puerto Rican is by recognizing distinct linguistic markers, by being familiar with the history of Latino populations in the Near Northwest side of Chicago (including Wicker Park but also the nearby West Town, Humboldt Park, and Logan Square), or by simply making an interpretive assumption and speculating that the character is a stand-in for the director herself.[31] There are specific filmic elements that make Evy's Puerto Ricanness difficult to grasp, and as a result, it is much easier to perceive Evy as a generic "Latina" than as a Puerto Rican, suggesting Troche's possible (perhaps unconscious) critical move away from nation-specific identities towards more pan-ethnic, collective ones, or a belief that Puerto Ricanness can be determined by simply looking at someone and hearing them speak Spanish, a tricky and imperfect test. Complicating this even further is the fact that Troche's own comments on her Puerto Rican heritage, frequently articulated in interviews, and her discussion of the importance of Migdalia Meléndez's Puerto Ricanness are often implicitly dismissed and/or not perceived as particularly relevant (or just simply unknown) by most people familiar with the film.

Go Fish has been celebrated by critics and audiences alike because of its low-key, fairly realistic, positive representations of what seem to be predominantly happy lesbian-of-color and white lesbian characters, at times engaging in sensuous lovemaking, in a film with catchy music including Cuban mambo as well as acoustic folk rock by Mila Drumke; fascinating lighting; unusual camera shots; and masterful experimental editing done by Troche herself. While the film is not easily read as Latina, it is an important document of our queer Latina Chicago history.

147

IV. *Circuitos de la memoria:* **Latina/o Queer History in Chicago**

A common denominator between the social and political organizing efforts of Latina lesbian organizations and the myriad Latina/o queer artistic proposals discussed in the previous section are the social intimacies they promote. These moments—from time spent together in a discussion group to the collective spectatorship of a film—are instances in our social history in need of documentation. But these practices of sharing also model the ways in which the archives of Latina/o queer history are continuously activated in the present. These collective pedagogies of the historical past are beautifully staged in the nightlife geographies of Latina/o queer club cultures.

It is a typical Thursday night in Chicago and a crowd of young queer Latina/o men, women, and other-gendered folk (as well as some straight friends and family members) wait in line at the entrance of Club Circuit, one of the largest dance clubs in Chicago's Boystown neighborhood. One by one they go through the ritual of the I.D. check, pay their cover, and extend their forearm toward the bouncer who stamps them with the temporary assurance of belonging to the night's social scene. It is "La Noche Loca," a weekly party advertised as "Chicago's longest running Latin night" and hosted by no other than La Cueva's grand dame Miss Ketty Teanga.[32] The evening features a diverse musical program as the DJ spins *cumbia*, hip-hop, *salsa*, *merengue*, and pop sets frequently enhanced by an add-on techno beat or a Latin house arrangement. It also showcases lip-synching performances by a rotating roster of Latina drag queens anchored by Miss Ketty's sharp wit and her typically flirtatious rapport with the audience.

Miss Ketty's girls rely on a repertoire of contemporary pop music both in English and Spanish. But every so often an old *bolero* or a pop song from the 1970s or 1980s, even the early 1990s, will sneak in and Miss Ketty will inquire from her audience whether they recognize or remember the song. She will often remark teasingly upon her audience's youth and school them on the appreciation of Latina/o queer anthems of yesteryear. This sixty-three-year-old pioneer of Chicago's Latina/o queer public culture and her fellow divas perform these songs to new generations of young audiences with incredible gusto and a passionate commitment. Their performances not only honor the shared experiences of Latina/o queer community in music and dance but stage for a new generation the labor of the drag queen as an important convener of this social scene.[33] Miss Ketty and her fellow queens participate in what scholar David Román has termed "archival drag" or performances that "set out to

Promotional flyer for party at Circuit Night Club, Chicago, June 2, 2010.

reembody and revive a performance from the past."[34] Miss Ketty's performances of history, invested as they are in accessing the archives of queer memory, transfer among the gathered youth knowledge about the ways we live, love, and struggle as queer Latinas/os. They also propel us to imagine our futures in a city where our presence is long-lived if little documented, where our beauty and creative wisdom is spectacularly displayed at clubs from La Cueva to Circuit as well as stages, airwaves, chapbooks, and posters and where we seek community and political solidarity in the intimacy of the potluck, the energizing chaos of the street rally, or the subtlety of the poem.

It is important to record the groundbreaking works of Miss Ketty Teanga, LLENA, Amigas Latinas, Achy Obejas, Rane Arroyo, Rose Troche, Coya Paz, Fausto Fernós and many others for the Latina/o queer archive. But it is just as important to circulate this archival knowledge to new generations who seek the wisdom of the past to imagine their queer futures. Much like a 1970s anthem song performed on "La Noche Loca" at Circuit, Latina/o queer history begs for invested, embodied, and yes, pleasurably witty engagements. Want to join the dance?

ENDNOTES

1. Important contributions in this respect include essays by Carlos Decena, Jessi Gan, Tim Retzloff, Horacio Roque Ramírez, and Salvador Vidal-Ortiz, plus anthologies such as *Compañeras: Latina Lesbians* edited by Juanita Ramos (New York City: Latina Lesbian History Project, 1987), *Chicana Lesbians: The Girls Our Mothers Warned Us about* edited by Carla Trujillo (Berkeley: Third Woman Press, 1991), and *Gay Latino Studies: A Critical Reader*, co-edited by Michael Hames-García and Ernesto Martínez (Durham: Duke University Press, 2011). Susana Peña's work on gay Cubans in Miami destabilizes the New York/San Francisco/Los Angeles triangle. Key books on Latina/o queer cultural production include Marivel Danielson's *Homecoming Queers: Desire and Difference in Chicana Latina Cultural Production* (New Brunswick, NJ: Rutgers University Press, 2009), Catriona Rueda Esquibel's *With Her Machete in Her Hand: Reading Chicana Lesbians* (Austin: University of Texas Press, 2006), Lawrence La Fountain-Stokes's *Queer Ricans: Cultures and Sexualities in the Diaspora* (Minneapolis: University of Minnesota Press, 2009) and Ricardo Ortiz's *Cultural Erotics in Cuban America* (Minneapolis: University of Minnesota Press, 2007).

2. This and all subsequent demographic figures are cited from Berenice Alejo, *The Latino Landscape: A Metro Chicago Guide and Non-Profit Directory* (South Bend, Ind.: The Institute for Latino Studies at the University of Notre Dame, 2008), 9.

3. Ibid., 10.

4. La Villita (also known as the Little Village or South Lawndale) is also the setting of Tadeo García's film *On the Downlow* (2004), which is about "the relationship between Isaac and Angel, two young Latinos involved in a Southside Chicago gang" (Gilberto Magaña, plot summary of *On the Downlow*, Internet Movie Database, www.imdb.com).

5. Kari Lydersen, "La Cueva: The Oldest Latino Drag Club in the Country Has Done Much to Change Attitudes in Chicago's Mexican Community," *Colorlines Magazine* (July 1, 2006): 49–50.

6. La Escuelita, a Latina/o dance club in New York City, began operations shortly after the Stonewall riots. See Manuel Guzmán, "'Pa La Escuelita Con Mucho Cuida'o y por la Orillita': A Journey through the Contested Terrains of the Nation and Sexual Orientation" in *Puerto Rican Jam: Essays on Culture and Politics,* eds. Frances Negrón-Muntaner and Ramón Grosfogel (Minneapolis: University of Minnesota Press, 1997), 209–28.

7. For an excellent discussion of La Cueva, especially the performances that take place there, see Achy Obejas's recent essay "Juanga Forever," *TriQuarterly Online* (July 5, 2010), accessed July 26, 2010, http://triquarterly.org/nonfiction/juanga-forever.

8. Marilyn Morales, interview by Lourdes Torres, February 27, 2010 and June 2009.

9. Carmen Abrego, interview by Lourdes Torres, January 29, 2010.

10. LLENA was committed to insuring that all their meetings were accessible to both monolingual Spanish-speaking and monolingual English-speaking women. All meeting minutes were issued in both Spanish and English.

11. Jamie Jimenez, interviewed by Lourdes Torres, November 21, 2008; Carmen Abrego, interviewed by Lourdes Torres, January 29, 2010; Marilyn Morales, interviewed by Lourdes Torres, February 27, 2010; and Amparo Jimenez, interviewed by Lourdes Torres, August 7, 2010.

12. See, for example, the writings by lesbian feminists of color in the United States such as Combahee River Collective, "A Black Feminist Statement," in Gloria Hull, Patricia Bell Scott, and Barbara Smith, eds. *All the Women Are White, All the Blacks Are Men But Some of Us Are Brave: Black Women's Studies* (Old Westbury; N.Y.: The Feminist Press, 1982); Cherríe Moraga and Gloria Anzaldúa, eds., *This Bridge Called My Back: Writings by Radical Women of Color* (Watertown, Mass: Persephone Press, 1981); *Home Girls: A Black Feminist Anthology* (New York: Kitchen Table: Women of Color Press, 1983); and Cherríe Moraga, *Loving in the War Years* (New York: Kitchen Table: Women of Color Press, 1983).

13. Carmen Abrego, interviewed by Lourdes Torres, January 29, 2010.

14. Quoted from LLENA minutes, Decemeber 12, 1989; also Carmen Abrego, interviewed by Lourdes Torres, January 29, 2010; and Amparo Jimenez, interviewed by Lourdes Torres, August 7, 2010.

15. Only one issue of the newsletter was published.

16. Mona Noriega, interviewed by Lourdes Torres, July 22, 2008; and Jamie Jimenez, interviewed by Lourdes Torres, November 21, 2008.

17. The reflections on LLENA's demise are by Marilyn Morales, Jamie Jimenez, Carmen Abrego, and Mona Noriega, interviewed by Lourdes Torres, various dates.

18. Mona Noriega, interviewed by Lourdes Torres, July 22, 2008; and Marilyn Morales, interviewed by Lourdes Torres, June 2009.

19. Tracy Baim's *Out and Proud in Chicago: An Overview of the City's Gay Community* (Chicago: Surrey Books, 2008) is the first book to document Chicago's queer history through a rich archive of photos and incisive essays by key journalists and scholars. The book is a companion piece to a documentary of the same name that explores the history of Chicago's lesbian, gay, bisexual, and transgender (LGBT) citizens from the Civil War to the present.

20. Evette Cardona (statement during question and answer period) at Out@CHM event, March 4, 2010.

21. Marilyn Morales, interviewed by Lourdes Torres, June 2009.

22. Amigas Latinas Focus Group report, 2006.

23. See Linda García Merchant, "From Ava Gardner to Mis Nalgas: The Story of Our Beautiful Brown Skinned Sexuality," *Diálogo* (Center for Latino Research of Depaul University) 12 (Summer 2009): 35–36.

24. See "Daniel Sotomayor," Chicago Gay and Lesbian Hall of Fame, http://www.glhalloffame.org/index.pl?item=26&todo=view_item. (accessed August 16, 2010).

25. Achy Obejas, *We Came All the Way from Cuba So You Could Dress Like This?* (Pittsburgh: Cleis Press, 1994); *Memory Mambo* (Pittsburgh: Cleis Press, 1996); and *Days of Awe* (New York: Ballantine Books, 2001).

26. Félix Padilla, *Latino Ethnic Consciousness: The Case of Mexican Americans and Puerto Ricans in Chicago* (Notre Dame, Ind.: University of Notre Dame Press, 1985) and *Puerto Rican Chicago* (Notre Dame, Ind.: University of Notre Dame Press, 1987); Ana Yolanda Ramos-Zayas, *National Performances: The Politics of Class, Race, and Space in Puerto Rican Chicago* (Chicago: University of Chicago Press, 2003); Nicholas de Genova and Ana Yolanda Ramos-Zayas, *Latino Crossings: Mexicans, Puerto Ricans, and the Politics of Race and Citizenship* (New York: Routledge, 2003).

27. Erika Gisela Abad, "¿La Voz de Quién?", *Diálogo* (Center for Latino Research of Depaul University) 12 (Summer 2009): 28–34.

28. Rane Arroyo, *Home Movies of Narcissus* (Tucson: University of Arizona Press, 2002); *How To Name a Hurricane* (Tucson: University of Arizona Press, 2005); Pale Ramón (Cambridge, Mass.: Zoland Books, 1998); *Same-Sex Seances* (Toledo, Ohio: New Sins Press, 2008); *The Singing Shark* (Tempe, Ariz.: Bilingual Press, 1996).

29. Rane Arroyo, "X, My Ex," in *How to Name a Hurricane,* 100–10.

30. For a more extensive analysis of *Go Fish*, see Lawrence La Fountain-Stokes, *Queer Ricans: Cultures and Sexualities in the Diaspora* (Minneapolis: University of Minnesota Press, 2009), 108–22.

31. See Gina Pérez, *The Near Near Northwest Side Story: Migration, Displacement, and Puerto Rican Families* (Berkeley: University of California Press, 2004).
32. See the Circuit's weekly events calendar: http://www.circuitclub.com. (accessed on August 17, 2010).
33. For a discussion of performance resource sharing in Latina/o queer clubs, see Ramón H. Rivera-Servera, "Choreographies of Resistance: Latina/o Queer Dance and the Utopian Performative ," *Modern Drama* 47, no. 2 (2004): 269–89.
34. David Román, *Performance in America: Contemporary U.S. Culture and the Performing Arts* (Durham, N.C.: Duke University Press, 2005), 140.

10/19